Book Launch
Date 19/10/22
Psalm
My help
which mad

G000245690

10/07/23

God Makes All Things Beautiful in His Time

Rita C. Joy Vincent
with Matthew Vincent

Faithbuilders Publishing

© Rita C. Joy Vincent and Matthew Vincent 2022

Faithbuilders Publishing
12 Dukes Court, Bognor Road,
Chichester, PO19 8FX, United Kingdom
www.faithbuilderspublishing.co.uk

ISBN: 978-1-913181-86-4

All rights reserved. No Part of this Publication may be reproduced, stored in a retrieval system, or transmitted in any form or by any means without the prior permission of the publisher.

British Library Cataloguing in Publication Data. A catalogue record for this book is available from the British Library

Unless otherwise stated all scripture quotation are taken from The Authorized (King James) Version of the Bible ('the KJV'), the rights in which are vested in the Crown in the United Kingdom, is reproduced here by permission of the Crown's patentee, Cambridge University Press.

Formatted by Faithbuilders Publishing
Cover by Esther Kotecha, EKDesign
Printed in the United Kingdom

Contents

Foreword

There are few things as captivating and inspiring as a story. Through other people's stories, we are able to get a ringside seat into their lives. We look into the windows of their pain and struggles and begin to understand what has made them who they are. This book is just that.

Rita tells the story of the pain, pleasure, trials and triumphs, setbacks and setups that have brought her where she is today. As you read this book, you will not only enjoy the storytelling, but you will learn valuable lessons for life.

You will begin to appreciate that God honours faith and tenacity, that you will never achieve your dreams without a steadfast faith in God. Another lesson, which will be a blessing, is that you will never succeed alone. Rita shows that there are people that God will send your way to help you along the journey of life.

Further still, you will see that every promise of God comes with a measure of resistance, challenge, and initial doubt. She tells about the faithfulness of God, as she got help from even the unlikeliest of people. God is indeed faithful to those who trust Him.

This book is indeed a textbook, for anybody who seeks to realise their life's calling and destiny. Read it prayerfully, and you will be inspired to reach the heights you were born to reach. Read On!

Frank Ofosu-Appiah

Bishop Frank Ofosu-Appiah is the founder and Senior Pastor of All Nations Church, Atlanta, Georgia. He is also the general overseer of the Livings Springs churches.

Preface

"GIVE EAR, O my people, to my law: incline your ears to the words of my mouth. I will open my mouth in a parable: I will utter dark sayings of old: which we have heard and known, and our fathers have told us. We will not hide them from their children, showing to the generation to come the praises of the LORD, and his strength, and his wonderful works that he hath done." (Psalm 78:1-4)

This book is written for all to read, regardless of the age, religion or race of the reader. It covers various stages of my life, from childhood up to the fulfilment of the promises that God gave me. The Bible bears witness to God's power to change lives dramatically, for His glory. We read of our father Abraham, the story of Joseph, and of Saul of Tarsus who became Paul the Apostle, along with many others. God hasn't changed, and He continues to work miracles in the lives of His people. What He did for my husband and I shows God's power to fulfil His promises, against all the odds, even in our day. When you start reading, you won't want to stop, until you finish the book and start again. Read joyfully!

Acknowledgements

I dedicate this account of what I have been through to the Lord God Jehovah. He alone deserves all the glory, praise and adoration. With gratitude, many thanks go to my dearest husband who helped me to write this book. Special thanks to men and women, young and old, who God sent into my life to help make it a joy and a success. Your good deeds are written about here, to inspire others. Nobody can do it alone. I am blessed and thankful to all those who have been part of my life.

In particular, I would like to thank all those who read through an early draft of the manuscript and made valuable suggestions and corrections. I thank Dr Meyer Van Rensburg, Mr Rod Vincent, the late Dr Curdell McLeod, Dr Femi Olowu, Pastor Cynthia Osei, the late Mr Arthur Vincent and Dr Ellen Hagan. I am also grateful for the recommendations that I received from Pastor Steve Armah, Pastor Enoch Tettey, Pastor Yaw Bamfo and Prophets Ron and Jane Jollif. Finally, I am so grateful to Bishop Frank Ofosu-Appiah for writing the foreword.

Introduction

Psalm 40:1-6 is a Scripture the Lord gave me, as I waited patiently for Him. I would read through it again and again, and even personalise it by mentioning my own name, imagining by faith a communication between me and the Lord God. I kept prophesying and making confession to myself saying: "I waited patiently on the LORD; and He inclined unto me, and heard my cry." This became my daily confession. The book of James encourages us to be doers of the word and not hearers only, deceiving our own selves. I therefore put into practice positive speaking, and spoke the right words at that time, so that in the end I would eat the fruit. (Job 6:25) "How forcible are right words!"

The sixth verse of Psalm 40 drew my attention and gave me revelation. I would love to explain why. "Mine ears hast thou opened" was a revelation to me. I believe God is close to me, because of the things He does for me daily. I love to revere and obey Him, and do whatever He tells me to do, whenever I hear His voice, because He has opened my spiritual ears. Except the Lord opens our ears, we cannot hear Him whenever He speaks to us personally. It's my sincere prayer, for whoever reads this book, that if your ears are not yet opened, the Lord will open your spiritual ears in the mighty name of the Lord Jesus. May we never be among those that have ears but cannot hear the precious voice of the Holy Spirit, the gift of God to those who are born again in Christ.

I will never forget the day, 22nd October 2009, when a word from the Lord dropped into my spirit. I read the book of Jeremiah chapter 30:1-2, which says, "Thus speaketh the Lord God of Israel, saying, write thee all the words that I have spoken unto thee in a book." The prompting of the Lord's word was so clear, that I quickly drew a circle round the verse and wrote down the date and time, so that I would not forget to do just what the Lord wanted me to do.

The next bibical text that came into my mind was Ecclesiastes chapter 3. "To everything there is a season, and a time to every purpose under the heaven: a time to be born and a time to die … a time to weep and a time to laugh; a time to mourn and a time to dance." The eyes of my understanding were opened as I read through to "He hath made everything beautiful in His time." At that point I asked the Lord for an explanation of verses 1-11. The reply of the Lord gave me the wisdom and understanding to choose the title of my book. This is the Lord's reply in my own words:

> God is the author of time, and He created mankind in His own image, to fulfill His purposes on earth. God has no beginning or end. Therefore no man can go ahead of God to do anything. We are His creation, made to rely on Him in all our growth and changes in life.

The time we spend waiting for God to fullfill His promises has never been easy, even from our father Abraham's time. Abraham and Sarah had to go through a long wait, with trials and temptations. Hagar bore Abram a son called Ishmael, through the arrangement of Sarai, after which the Lord changed their names to Abraham and Sarah. Abraham then settled his mind to trust and wait patiently for God to bring the promise of the birth of Isaac to pass. There is no testimony without a test! You therefore need to hear from the Lord to enable you to wait patiently on Him.

God sometimes delays the answers to our prayers, until it may look impossible for them to be answered. Yet He is still working behind the scenes, to bring His promises to fulfillment. I have written my own testimony, to encourage you not to give in to the temptation to doubt God. If you keep trusting Him, He will come through for you.

We see the pattern of God waiting, until all human hope looks futile, throughout the scriptures. After Joseph saw in a dream his brothers and parents bowing before him, for many years it must have seemed to him ever more unlikely that his dream was being fulfilled. The very opposite of God's favour and blessing appeared to be his lot! Having been sold into slavery, he endured false accusation, imprisonment, and must have felt abandoned and powerless. Yet God was with him.

There is a great danger of not only despair, but bitterness and self pity, as we wait for God to answer our prayers. Sarah laughed at the promise of the Lord, that in her old age she would give birth to a son. It is clear from the context, when we read the biblical account, that this was not a laugh of joy. The Lord asked her why she laughed, and she denied that she had.

In my own life, there were many occasions when I could have turned to bitterness or despair. Before God fulfilled His promise to give me a husband, I did not have the things that the world counts as important. I often did not have paid employment and had to trust God to provide for me on a daily basis. I had no home of my own, and even my right to be in the U.K. was disputed. At one point, I even put my last pound coin into the offering!

In the New Testament, we read that Zechariah doubted the promise of the angel Gabriel, that he would give birth to a son in his old age, and was made dumb until the time that the promise was fulfilled. It is easy for us too to lose faith, when it seems that aspects of our own life have become barren. But nothing is impossible for God.

When the Lord Jesus heard that Lazurus was sick, He stayed where He was two more days. He only came to Mary and Martha after their brother had already died. What bitterness and disappointment, what heartbreak they must have felt. Why did the Lord wait? Why does He sometimes wait in our own trials, until it seems too late to us in our human reasoning? The Lord Himself tells us in John chapter 11 verse four: "When Jesus heard that, He said, This sickness is not unto death, but for the glory of God, that the Son of God might be glorified thereby."

It was for God's glory! He has given me a testimony and if you are a believer in the Lord Jesus Christ He is giving you a testimony as well. Not a testimony for your own honour, not an account of your own ability, not a story of your wisdom and goodness. No. An account of His power, faithfulness, love and mercy. And even if you are not a believer yet, please be assured that God has a testimony for you too. If you come to know Him, He will reveal His plans and purposes for you. That all may know that our God is a deliverer, and He gives beauty for ashes. When the Lord called Lazarus by name, and he rose from the dead, God did a miracle for which there was no human explanation and which glorified nobody but God.

I sincerely urge you to be aware and acknowledge that, after God gives you a word of promise, or a vision, or dream, His word will try you. (Psalm 105:19) As one of God's people who is truly born again in Christ, you may have received a prophecy, vision, or a promise from the Lord. The only way you can see the promise or vision fulfilled is to believe, have faith in God, focus on the Lord alone, and wait patiently for Him throughout your tests and trials. God will turn things around in your favour and bring everything to a beautiful end. He did it for me, He will surely do it for you too. This book is my testimony of waiting on God for twenty-eight years and trusting Him despite many challenges. As I have seen Him fulfill His promises, I hope you will agree that its title is appropriate: "God makes all things beautiful in His time!"

Chapter 1
Childhood

My mother told me the story of how remarkable my birth was. According to her, after the birth of my elder brother she had a miscarriage with her next baby. I was five and a half months hidden in her womb, and she was confirmed pregnant in her sixth month. On the day of my delivery, I was giggling with unusual smiles, which everyone around me commented on: "What a beautiful smiling baby!" There were British missionary midwives who worked in the hospital in Apam, my hometown, and they were all so happy and joyful about my birth. Later in life, God gave me a new name, Joy. But that aspect of my character was apparent to all, even from my birth.

Apam, which is joined to Winneba, is a small town in the central region of Ghana. The dialect spoken there is Fante, my native tongue and the name of my tribe. I lived there to the age of six, with my younger twin brothers, my mum, my grandmother, and my great grandmother, who lived to one hundred and ten. My older brother was away at boarding school. We could see the sea, as we looked out of our windows, as well as the houses made of mud and straw. Our own home was made of bricks and cement, with a toilet outside. We used to play on the beaches, near the fishermen and the women selling the fish. I attended a primary school that I could walk to. I remember seeing chickens, sheep and goats wandering everywhere. We awoke to the sound of cock crow and bird song. There were coconut trees and palm trees planted all around our home, as well as along the beaches, giving us a supply of fresh fruit throughout the year. We also drank koko every morning, which is made from ground maize. Roasted ground maize is often referred to as Tom Brown. And there was always fufu, a staple in Ghana, made from cassava and unripe plantain. We often ate it with palm nut soup, made from ground palm kernels. In those days, there were not many cars. We did a lot of walking. I remember how we gathered with our neighbours, in different houses, and all ate together as if we were one big family.

We attended a Methodist church every Sunday, and my mother was a chorister. Because of that, we had to go to church very early. My daddy lived in Accra, as he had seperated from my mother. When I was six, I went to live with my dad, as he had remarried. My brothers did not join us immediately, they stayed in Apam with my mum. I have good memories of my stepmother: she taught me how to cook and look after a home, so I could help care for my brothers when they came to join us. Because I was my father's only daughter, he loved to take me to the salon, to have my hair weaved, and bought me lovely clothes to wear.

When I was about twenty years of age, I noticed that my right foot had a scar close to my little toe. I asked my mother what happened. She replied, "I have mentioned it before but you might have forgotten." She then narrated how I had just begun to crawl, and was left sleeping on a mat late one afternoon. She was at home alone and needed to go to the outside toilet. She believes that I must have woken suddenly and, seeing nobody, began to crawl to where a kettle had been left full of boiling water. She said she could never forget that I kicked the kettle, and some drops of boiling water fell on my tiny right foot. She came running back when she heard me screaming like never before. She immediately rushed me to the hospital. Fortunately, the hospital was about half a mile from our home. According to her, my daddy blamed her and did not talk to her for months. They only resumed talking to each other when the wound was healed and I started to walk normally. As I write my story, I wish that Mum and Dad were alive for me to thank them for what happened. As you read on, you will find out what happened later concerning my burnt foot, and the reason for my gratitude towards them.

My daddy was very fond of me, because I was his only daughter among three brothers, and I was named after his

16

dad. Dad was born on the 31st October and I was born on the 30th October. I was told my grandfather was a generous giver and even gave to a fault, giving things away and looking for them later. He was known as Nana Kofi Mensah, and I was traditionally named Nana Aba Mensimah, in addition to my other names, Rita and Claudia. My dad said my name Rita was connected to a picture of a beautiful woman, used as the cover on a talcum powder he used daily. He really loved the perfumed scent of the powder, and he told my mum if she gave birth to a girl he would call her Rita. He said I would grow up to be beautiful like the woman on the powder container. Wasn't that funny?

As a child, I did the best I could to care for everybody around me. In school, I made friends easily because I was always smiling. I was chosen as the school prefect and had a good report at the end of each term. However, I recall an incident that occurred when I was in the preparatory school, aged only eight or nine. One morning, I told some of my dormitory mates that I saw, as in a vision, that the school bus had been involved in an accident, but no one was hurt. I was in the boarding house, and the school bus brought the day pupils from their homes every day, and both day and boarding pupils studied together. Not long after I had told them this, news reached the boarding house that the school bus had had an accident, but that no one had been hurt.

One of my classmates quickly went and told the Headmaster and Mistress of the school. I did not know who went and reported me, but I was called immediately to confirm the report. I affirmed the report and was asked to go home and bring my parents. That is a memory I will never forget. I remember my dad had travelled abroad, so I returned with my mother. What I do not remember now, was whether I was able to tell my mum exactly what had happened. Back at the boarding house with my mum, and after some disscussion with the Heads of the school, I was told to be careful and stop saying things like that, to avoid people calling me a witch. After this incident, I was silenced. How I wish my mother had taken notice of God's hand upon my life, but I was left alone. I would encourage all parents to watch over their young children with care. Prayerfully seek and inquire of the Lord with regard to your children's future.

I proceeded to Aggrey Memorial Zion College, in Cape Coast. I became the Bell Girl from Form Two, till I completed Form Five. I was the first to wake up, have my bath, get dressed , and ring the bell for the whole college. It is amazing that I did that for four years. After completing my O Levels, I desired to be a bilingual secretary, so I attended bilingual secretarial training for one year. I then changed to a Diploma course, studying hairdressing and beauty culture for another year. Beauty was something I loved, and not for myself alone. I loved beautifying others. It was many years later that I fully understood why I had changed to the beauty course. Whilst I was waiting for my residence permit to live and work in the UK, I was able to bless others with my hairdressing skills.

Immediately after my graduation from the school of hairdressing and beauty culture in 1981, I travelled to Nigeria to work as a Beautician. Fortunately for me, my cousin had a friend who was returning to Nigeria from Ghana and was able to give me a lift. I had a comfortable journey.

Chapter 2

Rescued From Armed Robbers

When I arrived in Nigeria, my cousin took me to the home of some distant relatives, and we both lived with them for some time. I did much of the cooking and cleaning while I stayed there. We both started looking for work, which my cousin found before I did. Lagos is a teeming city, full of hustle and bustle, where everyone seems to be buying and selling. The traffic is very heavy, and people are often stuck in "go slows". So people leave home early in the morning. You could hear the sound of traffic and car horns blowing all the time. The houses are close together. It is a hectic, crowded, but exciting city to live in. You have to be strong to live there. It felt like there was never an end to a day, or an end to a night. Everywhere, you could hear the sound of the Muslim call to prayer, competing with the sound of traffic and the sound of generators. Everyone who could afford one had a generator, as there were constant power cuts. Those who didn't have generators used old cans, with a wick coming out of a hole in the top. The fuel in the can was kerosene, also called paraffin. Where I was living we had lanterns, which we had to light each evening. There was also a constant shortage of water: I had to wash using only one cup. We had enough to eat, buying our food in the local markets. We ate a lot of beans, and Eba, which is made of Gari and eaten with spinach stew. Gari is made from dried cassava dough. We travelled by Molue, which are small buses, seating about thirty or forty people, or Danfo, which were mini-buses. They were often ancient! I don't think they had any insurance, or seat belts. They would stop anywhere, if you flagged them down, regardless of any vehicles behind them. It seemed that nobody obeyed the law.

After a few months, I found a good job on Victoria Island, in Lagos. I worked at the big Federal Palace Hotel, in a beauty salon. There were fifteen employees, (four men and eleven women), all young, in our twenties, working shifts. Some started early in the morning, and others late in the afternoon. I was blessed with long hair. As a beautician, I made sure I was smartly dressed, with a beautiful hair style to impress my clients. I captured the admiration of many clients, especially the wife of the Vice President of Nigeria, Mrs Beatrice Ekwenmeh, and other top politician's wives. I loved going the extra mile. For example, I served them with soft drinks and sometimes walked them to their cars, carrying their bags. Without being aware of it, I was always wearing a smile on my face, which earned me a lot of tips. At the end of every month, the total amount of my tips was always more than my salary. Owing to my joyful appearance, my clients booked me in advance. Sometimes, I was asked to work even when I was off duty. I found favor with the owner of the salon, who gave me a newly built house near her detached mansion, to live in free of charge. She was so generous and kind to me. Let me tell you how her kindness towards me, in giving me a home, saved her life from armed robbers.

Armed robbers wrote to the salon owner, warning her that, on a particular date and time, she would be robbed. This was the norm in Nigeria in those days. Once you received a letter from them, you could be sure that they would turn up. In the letter, you were warned to vacate your house, to avoid confrontation, and also told to leave all your jewellery and money where they could be found, in order to save your life. It was a period when the rich lived in fear in Lagos. The salon owner took their warning very seriously, and reported the armed robbers to the authorities. When the day came, she did exactly as she was told by leaving her mansion gate and doors open, and alerted the police that the robbers were arriving after midnight. That night she asked to come and hide under my bed for protection. Just after midnight, we heard the armed robbers discussing loudly if they should enter my room. But one of them said I was a Ghanaian working at the salon, and that they should leave me alone. So they went straight to the mansion and robbed it. The police blocked the road, and the robbers were arrested and later sent to jail. My employer received back her stolen goods. She was so grateful and happy that her life was spared.

The atmosphere at work was always busy, creative and fullfilling. Such was my youthful heyday! I hardly had time to attend any church services. In 1983, a political issue arose unexpectedly. Ghanaians without residence permits were asked to leave and go back to their own country.This was possibly a pay back for what Ghana did to Nigeria some years before. In those days, one only needed a passport and a yellow vaccination card, which enabled one to travel in and out of the neighbouring countries such as Togo, Benin, Nigeria and Ivory Coast, in and around West Africa. In no time I found myself a victim, because I was working without a residence permit. Trouble visited me. Someone reported me to the immigration authorities. One afternoon, as I was working, I was led out of work by two immigration officers into a prison truck, not knowing where they were taking me. The prison truck was painted black, and was known in Nigeria, and elsewhere, as a black maria. You couldn't see anything from the inside, apart from through a few small windows with iron bars. I felt very alone and fearful. The immigration officers didn't question me, but said that I would be interrogated when I arrived at my destination.

Unbeknown to me, there was a well-known Ghanaian politician staying in the hotel, who knew all about me and who saw me being pushed into the prison truck. He acted quickly on my behalf, and called the Ghana High Commissioner who came to rescue me at a place called Alabon Close. Thankfully, as soon as we arrived, I saw a black Mercedes Benz car with the Ghanaian flag, and I found myself returning with the Ghanaian High Commissioner. What a miracle the Almighty God wrought for me, though I did not even know Him then. After that incident, I was advised by the salon owner to stay away from work for some time, so I left Lagos and travelled to the northern part of Nigeria, where my elder brother lived and worked. It was an opportunity for me to get to know other parts of Nigeria.

Where I went to live was sparsely populated. I lived in Yola, which was in Gongola state. The houses were very different to those in Lagos: They were round huts, made of mud, with straw on the roofs, and were so low you had to bend down to enter. These huts looked small from the outside, but were quite spacious when you went inside. Nobody cooked in the main huts, where they slept, as they had separate huts for cooking. People didn't use chairs, they sat on mats on the floor. Although the weather in that part of Nigeria can be very hot, the huts stayed nice and cool. The roads were basic and uneven. Outside of the towns, they were largely dirt tracks. During the dry season, by the time that you finished your journey your hair was covered by dust, unless your car had air conditioning.

There were animals everywhere: goats, sheep, cows, guinea fowl, chickens and hens. Herdsmen looked after them, and milked the cows every morning. The milk would often be bartered locally, though some was taken to the main market to be sold. People were kind, and often gave me food and milk. They were generous and welcoming to strangers. There was plenty of food for everyone. People grew okro, tomatoes, spinach, maize and millet. The people in the area were mainly Muslim, though there were Christians as well. The main tribe was Fulani, and they loved to teach me their language, Hausa, and tribal dialect, Fufude. At that time I learnt to speak Hausa well, though I have largely forgotten it now. I remember how beautiful the Fulani women looked, with their jewellery and colourful clothes. They always wore headscarfs, and wore their hair long.

After a few weeks of staying with my brother, I met a Muslim man who showed me much love and took an interest in me. I was only twenty-three years old and had no experience of any kind of relationship. I did not know the difference between Christianity, Hinduism, Buddhism and Islam. All that I knew was the Methodist Church I attended with my parents, who were both choristers. Only God knew why this man, who was often called Alhaji, (the title used by Muslims who had made a pilgrimage to Mecca) had come into my life. He was rich and looked very handsome. Things quickly changed around me, as he won an election and gave me the opportunity to be his receptionist. He helped me to settle down in a well furnished house, as well as providing money for me to purchase the equipment needed for a new salon in the North. However, within three months of his reign as a governor beginning, he was arrested and imprisoned following a coup d'etat. His imprisonment came as a shock to all who knew him. Had the Alhaji not been imprisoned, I could have ended up marrying him, to become the fourth of his wives. It was not meant to be. I thank God!

Chapter 3
Obedience To My Call

I waited for the Alhaji for almost a year following his sudden imprisonment, considering walking out on him but reluctant to do so as he had been so generous and kind to me. I did not have any savings after shopping and renting a place, and did not know exactly what to do, nor was there any one to advise me. I was by myself, because my brother had finished his contract and returned to Ghana. At that point things became hard and unbearable for me, so I returned to Lagos to live with friends, hoping that the Alhaji would soon be released from prison.

My hope was restored one morning, when the news came on the Nigerian television. I heard that some politicians had been released and that he was one of them. After his release, he was so pleased and expressed how much he appreciated my patience and faithfulness in waiting for him. For my reward, he asked me to look for a place of my own. It was a great relief after staying with friends here and there with much suffering. I found a newly built flat which cost 5000 naira. I could rent it for five years. The Alhaji gave me half the money as a deposit, and asked me to come for the balance in a week's time. I paid the deposit to the landlord, with an agreement that I would return with the balance.

On one fateful day, in October 1985, I went back to collect the balance. I do not know what went so terribly wrong, for the same man who was so happy to see me after his release from prison to turn his back on me, calling me a mad woman. He had suddenly changed towards me, and harshly demanded to know why I was following him. He did not give me the balance for the flat, but told me to get out of his house and that he never wanted to see my face again. Unbelievable! Words will not be enough to express how I felt. I even thought I was mad. Oh! Alas! Man will always fail you. As we read in Jeremiah chapter 17:5, "Thus saith the LORD; Cursed be the man that trusted in man, and maketh flesh his arm, and whose heart departed from the LORD."

As I left his house I said to myself, "I am finished! What am I going to do?" However, though I did not know it at the time, that moment proved to be a turning point in my life. That event kept me from going the wrong way, and led me to the path and plan God had for me. I decided to go and collect my money, and travel back to Ghana as soon as I could. I thought I could re-establish my life in Ghana. However, when I got to the landlord and I told him my predicament, he started laughing, saying, "I thought as much." So I asked him why he said that. His reply was that when I brought the deposit and mentioned the Alhaji's name, the name of a prominent political figure who was well known for his many wives, he wondered why a beautiful young lady like me would get involved with such a man. He then asked me, "Are you a Muslim?" My answer was no. That was the start of a lot of changes in my life.

The landlord only agreed to give me back the money if he took a hundred naira for his reward. He said I had broken a "bridge of contract". I did not understand what he meant by breaking a bridge of contract, but I thought if I only got the 2400 naira back that was still a lot of money. As he was giving me back the money, I will always recall his expression of sympathy, as I looked straight at him. He then asked me if I would like to follow him to a church, where a prophet in the church would reveal to me what had gone wrong between me and the Alhaji, and also tell me if he was my rightful husband. I actually wanted to know what went wrong, because I felt so hurt and disappointed by the Alhaji. I felt I had no choice but to agree to follow this man to the church, called Celestia Church of Christ.

It was the first time in many years that I had entered a church. I had never heard of this church before. For about five years, I had been so preoccupied with my hairdressing business and the Alhaji. I did not have time to seek God in my youthful heyday. (Ecclesiastes 12:1, "Remember now thy Creator in the days of thy youth, while the evil days come not nor the years draw nigh, when thou shalt say, I have no pleasure in them.") I was about twenty-five years old, and the decision to follow the landlord to the church turned my life around. As we got closer to the church, he pointed and said I should go in alone, because he had a lot of work to do. He directed me to buy a candle as I entered, and speak quietly to God. He urged me not to be afraid, but to pray and ask God whatever I wanted to know concerning my life, and the prophet would give me all the answers. As I sat quietly alone in a corner on a bench, with the candle close to my lips, confused and feeling rejected, I became so curious about what answers I would receive from God.

When the prophet came, I was the seventh in line, but he called me first, by showing me signs of grief and hurt. He spoke in Yoruba, a common language in Nigeria. Another person started interpreting in English. He said I should kneel down and shout "Alleluia" seven times, as a sign of victory, because it was the Almighty God who had ordered my steps to the church. He said it was the day of my salvation. God had revealed to him that I was His chosen prophetess to the world. He then revealed what happened when I was in the preparatory school, about the incident of the school bus which I had known was going to crash. I was almost scared, but he immediately cautioned me not to be afraid, because the God who had called me would always be with me. He also mentioned how I felt that I had been silenced as a child, but he said that God was preparing me, and cautioned that I still had a long way to go with God. He did not reveal anything particular about the Alhaji, but he said all that I went through with much suffering was not the plan of God for me. Finally, he told me that my current intention was to go back to Ghana, but God said I should not go back, until He opened the door for me to travel in His time. Rather, from then on I should start sleeping in the church for God's protection, and attend church services. I said to myself, how can I sleep in a church I know nothing about? However, after hearing the words of the prophet, I sensed that God was really watching over me. I therefore decided to obey God and receive His protection. Everything about the church was new and strange to me, and I found it diffcult to think about what to do. Now, after thirty years of accepting the higher call of God, I can truly say that God is real, and those who wait upon Him will never be ashamed, either in this life or the next.

Chapter 4
New Life In Celestial Church Of Christ

I began sleeping in the church as the prophet had told me to. Gradually, I learnt from different people in 'Cele', as the church was often called, and conformed to their way of life. Their dress code still stands out to this day, and they are recognised as a white garment church. The members of the church, when wearing their white garments, always walk with bare feet. They have a branch in Peckham, London. (I once lived in Peckham with my brother.) As I am writing, I wonder if they still walk with bare feet whenever they wear their white garments during the winter period, for who can stand the cold weather in bare feet? I remember my days in Cele, and I thank God for His grace that helped me to come out in His time. I attended services three days a week including Sundays.

Celestia Church of Christ had various branches, and every individual church was in a particular parish. In the services, men and women sat separately. Prophets would frequently minister to individuals. They often made mention of angels, calling on the angel Gabriel or Michael to help people. The prophets taught that it was the angels that brought messages from God. All this sounded very strange to me. The branch that I lived in was in a walled enclosure. To enter, you went in through a large gate into a spacious compound with the church building at the centre. There were also blocks of flats around the edge of the compound with many people living in them, including the "Shepherd" of the church. I didn't have a great deal of contact with him, but found him friendly and respectful when I did speak to him. The workers in the church shared the flats but had their own rooms. A number of prophets also lived there. There was always a prophet available for ministry. The church workers and prophets also had houses in nearby towns.

There were a number of us who were sleeping at the church for protection. The men slept in one corner of the church, away from the women. After a service finished, we put the chairs away and put our blankets on the floor with a pillow, which we had to provide ourselves. I didn't make friends, I minded my own business, but there was one church worker with whom I found favour. He introduced me to his wife and children. His wife kindly suggested that I use her husband's room to sleep in, so that I wouldn't have to sleep on the floor, and that he stay at the family home during the time of my protection. It was a pleasure to be able to cook my own food again in the kitchen of his flat. Every Sunday, and sometimes during the week, someone would do a thanksgiving celebration at the church. People celebrated birthdays, or gave thanks to God for special blessings. They would bring food and drink; jollof rice and chicken or beef stew, as well as fruit. That meant there was always food available. At other times, people would just buy fruit and put it in the storehouse to bless the people living at the church. After some time, I started to buy fruit for the storehouse myself, and the Shepherd prophesied that I would never lack fruit in my home. My husband and I can testify that this prophecy has been fulfilled!

Slowly, a month in my new enviroment passed, and I was still wondering why God did not tell me anything about the Alhaji. I therefore decided to ask God through the prophet once again. I bought a candle, and quietly prayed and asked God if the Alhaji was to be my husband. I was uncertain why God wanted me to remain in Nigeria and not to return to Ghana. I saw the same prophet, and this time he asked a volunteer to write down my message. He said God was showing him a vision of a "noble man", meaning someone with a good heart. He also said that he could see me kneeling beside this man at the altar, and that God himself was adding His blessing. He concluded the message by saying that God had called me to bless me, so that I would also be a blessing to many. I did not understand the vision and the message. However, I continued to stay at the church, recovering from all that I went through, not knowing what the next day would bring. Over the years, I forgot all about the vision of the noble man, and continued to think that one day the Alhaji would call me back. It took many years for me to stop thinking about him.

After six months of living at the church, the Shepherd (the senior leader of the parish) told me my protection was over. I should therefore find somewhere else to stay, and continue to come to church. By this time, my money was almost finished. Fortunately for me, a very good friend of mine called Happy, who once lived with me while I was working in the salon, gave me a room in her house. It was as if God went ahead to prepare that place for me. I visited some other churches, such as Redeemed Church of God, Deeper Life, Latter Rain, Assemblies of God, Cherubim and Seraphim (another type of Celestia Church of Christ), and Household Fellowship in Lagos.

Reflecting on the day I stepped into Cele, I began to feel that God had called me for a purpose. The family and friends I knew before my higher call did not understand me. Stories of different kinds were told about me. I was no longer the ever busy beautician working in the Grand Hotel. I was now walking with bare feet, in a long white gown, with a head cap to match. My daily routine was going about preaching the Gospel. I used to preach on the street, and sometimes on the Moules, (minibuses that are used for public transport). I did draw a crowd at times, but sometimes people would try and shut me down, telling to go back to my own country to preach. They recognised from my accent that I was Ghanaian. I preached on my own. I told people the Gospel, to give their life to Master Jesus, as much as I understood the Gospel at the time. When my family heard about it, they thought I was mad. News reached my family that I was walking about in Lagos, speaking and laughing and doing nothing for a living.

I believe this was the enemy of our souls at work. Right from the day God delivered me from the Alhaji's hand and brought me into the church, Satan the adversary of mankind began operating against my life. But the Lord took me through a learning process to help me to know Him well. (Matthew 11:28-30, "Come unto me all ye that labor and are heavy laden, and I will give you rest. Take my yoke upon you, and learn of me; for I am meek and lowly in heart: and ye shall find rest unto your soul.") Indeed, at this point of my life I needed 'rest' for my soul. By the grace of God I grew in passion, seeking after the ways of the Lord. I was noted in Cele for addressing the Lord as Master Jesus. I learnt that from my mother who always addressed Him as such. In no time people were refering to me as 'Master Jesus', because whenever I spoke, I mentioned Master Jesus and not just Jesus as other people around me addressed Him. I thought, why do people just mention Jesus, as though He were their equal mate, without any reverence for His sovereignty. (Even king David in the Old Testament addressed Him as Lord: "THE LORD said to my Lord, Sit thou at my right hand, until I make thine enemies thy footstool." Psalm 110:1)

One day a guest speaker was invited to preach. He opened the floor after the sermon for any questions. A lady member of the church I was living with (I was then working for her as a house help) stood up and asked if it was right for someone to mention the name of the Lord Jesus, as many as a hundred times in a day. The speaker's reply was that the Lord Jesus is the Saviour of the world, so His name can be mentioned at any time, even a thousand times a day, if we need to call on Him for help. When we returned home, the lady told me to leave her house the next day. What a surprise! When I left her house, I had nowhere to go, so I went to an old friend who had a salon. As I told her about my experience, a lady client of my friend offered to help me. She took me to her house and gave me a room to sleep in. She was so kind that I could not believe it. I told her I loved cleaning, so she allowed me to clean her house the next day.

When she returned from work, and found her home well cleaned and everything beautifully arranged, she promised to take me out shopping at the weekend. We went out that

Saturday morning and she bought me new clothes and shoes and in the evening we went out for dinner. When we returned, she asked me to come and sleep with her. I was shocked. That was how she revealed who she was. She said she really loved me and would do everything to help me, but I refused to sleep with her. She told me to get out of her house the following day. She also took all the shopping back. Thankfully, my very kind friend Happy, with whom I had left some of my belongings, let me return to stay with her.

It was one trial after another, and even persecution after I took a neighbour to church. A lady called Comfort, who lived near to my friend Happy, asked me to take her to Cele. She wanted to hear from God, as I had mentioned my experience to her. Many people came from far and wide to hear from God. I was also informed, by people in the parish, that the prophet who gave me the message was genuine and truly heard from God. I had no doubts about him. So I took her to the prophet, and afterwards we both attended the evening service. The sermon preached was about any man or woman living together unmarried. As we read in Hebrews 13:4, "Marriage is honourable in all, and the bed undefiled: but whoremongers and adulterers God will judge." It was the first time I had heard that message, which caused me to greatly fear God. After the service, Comfort and I returned home safely.

The next day, as I was going out, Comfort's boyfriend suddenly attacked me. He pulled me forcefully, removing my glasses which I had been wearing for eighteen years. He broke them in pieces and gave me a slap to the face which brought stars to my eyes. Comfort later explained that they were not married, so she had decided not to sleep with her boyfriend until he married her, or paid the dowry to her family. The boyfriend said I was the reason for her decision. What an expensive price to pay for taking someone to church!

A week after the incident, during an evening service, a prophetess came to me with a word from the Lord. She said that I should not worry about my broken glasses and whatever I had suffered for His name's sake. I was really surprised that she knew about my broken glasses. She said God would give me an eye with which I would be able to see what others cannot see. She also gave me a prophecy that I would be called by many good names. A distant uncle, who I once lived with in Lagos, explained to me what the prophetess meant by an eye to see what others cannot see. From then on, I decided not to wear glasses but to walk by faith. Thank God for His faithfulness, for the Lord has fullfilled His promise of giving me an eye to see. (The gift of discernment). I have not yet come across anyone who suffered for Christ's sake who has not been blessed by God. The Lord is a great rewarder of those that remain faithful in suffering for His name's sake. Whatever persecution you are going through is never hidden from God, just endure it and give Him thanks. It might be difficult at the present moment, but you will rejoice in the end. (Psalm 126:5, "They that sow in tears shall reap in joy.")

My days in Cele finally came to an end as I grew in the Lord and became fed up walking with bare feet and wearing a white garment. I did not restrict myself to Cele alone, but kept visiting other churches. No one told me to stop attending Cele, but I decided to attend a church where I was free to wear a beautiful dress, and to wear shoes. The Lord gave me this understanding as I hungered for righteousness. I burnt all the white garments, including my special loincloth which signfied that I was seen as a prophetess of God in Cele. I felt that if God called me as His own prophetess, then I did not need that special loincloth but could be used by God anywhere. One very important event at Cele, which I escaped, was the baptism in the sea at the end of every year for all new members. I was in my monthly period, and that prevented me from wearing my white garment at that time. The steps of the righteous are ordered by the Lord. Moreover the prophet that gave me the messages from God had left the church. I felt a burden had been lifted from my shoulders as I walked freely out of Celestia Church of Christ.

During my days in Cele, the founder died, leaving behind so many wives and children. I did ponder on God's Word in first Timothy chapter three verse two: "A bishop then must be blameless, the husband of one wife." However, I believe God did lead me there for training and learning. It was not for me to judge, but in the end He brought me out in His own time. Nothing before its time! God gave me revelation through the story of Joseph and Mary, the mother of our Lord Jesus. I read that God sent His only begotten Son to Egypt for safety. After the death of Herod, the family returned to Israel. The Lord permitted me to attend Cele for a time, to learn about different churches and to find out where I really belonged and would learn sound biblical doctrines.

Chapter 5

His Lordship

I moved out of the house of my friend Happy to live with my distant uncle. My problems with accommodation continued, as I was sleeping on a carpet in his living room. During this period, I bought the book of Psalms and used it daily in my prayers. The book contained guidance about which Psalms could best be used to pray for specific needs. For example, if one is having trouble sleeping, Psalm 23 is a good psalm to use in prayer before bed. The first time I saw the book I loved it, because it contained so many prayers that were relevant to me. I could spend three hours just reading the book as I knelt in prayer. My daily routine became praying and talking to God. I saw many answers to prayer, but after a year I felt led to move on so that I did not become reliant on one particular book.

I still have many Psalms committed to memory, which is a great blessing to me, especially Psalm 40 which the Lord gave me to help me to wait upon Him. I sought the Lord with all my heart and continuously asked God to reveal Himself to me, just as He did to Mary Magdalene. Early one morning, the Lord revealed Himself to me in a manner which I will never forget. On the wall of the living room was a picture of my Lord Jesus. As I knelt down praying, I fell into a trance. I saw the picture of my Lord Jesus coming down from the wall towards me, as if I was watching a movie. As I looked, wondering what was happening to the picture, I saw my Saviour appearing real and alive from behind the picture and standing right in front of me. I held His feet tightly and said I would not let Him go, but He spoke to me with a sweet gentle voice saying, "My daughter, I came to let you know that I am your Lord, and I am alive forever. It was necessary for Me to go, so that I would send My Holy Spirit to come and dwell in you." I replied: "Amen", because the vision was so real. I felt the Master's feet. After that encounter, I could not remain the same or mention Jesus without saying Lord. He became so real to me that I wanted to address Him always by His Holy name, Lord Jesus. The effect of His Lordship in my life is that I believe He owns me, because He bought me with His precious blood that was shed on the Cross of Calvary. I also publicly confessed Him as my personal Saviour, which seals the covenant for every individual who accepts Him as Lord.

Chapter 6
Return To Ghana

In 1988, the Lord opened the door for me to return to Ghana. One day I received a message that the Alhaji wanted to see me. It was about three years since I had last seen or heard from him. I had forgotten all about him and was minding my higher calling as I went out and preached the Gospel. I greatly wondered what he wanted from me. I only decided to go so that I could preach the Gospel to him. I arrived at his office after midday. He was filled with smiles as soon as he saw me. He started telling me he had heard all about me, and how I went about preaching. He confessed that he knew I was a changed person, though he could not understand what had changed me and caused me to preach the Gospel. Thankfully, I was able to tell him about my calling and encouraged him to consider giving his life to Christ. Towards the end of our conversation, he said he felt that I should go home to my family for a break. He then gave me 3500 naira for my flight and spending money. I reminded him that I still had some belongings in Yola, in the north, but he said I should leave those and go back to Ghana. He wouldn't permit me to collect them at that time. I learnt from this experience that God can use any person to meet a need. Also, that one must be content with any help received from God through man. The Alhaji only met my need because of the plan of God. God is the ultimate source of all provision. ("The earth is the Lord's and the fullness thereof", Psalm 24:1). I left him, rejoicing that a seed was sown into his life.

My family were all amazed to see me, especially my mother. She said she had wanted to come and get me but could not afford the air fare for both of us. She was a bit cautious, and carefully listened to me, when she first saw me. After three days of my staying with her, she became convinced I was in sound mind and good health. Both my parents were still Methodist Christians, as far as I knew, though they were separated and lived apart. My daddy told me how his concern for me had led him to a local herbalist, a seer, because of the negative report he had received about me from Nigeria. He narrated how as soon as he got to the herbalist, and my name was mentioned, the herbalist told my daddy that he could see fire around me. He then said my daddy should go away from him. Praise the Lord, Alleluia! The Lord showed Himself so strong for me even in my absence, and just at the mention of my name. From what my dad told me, I learnt that God sets a wall of fire around His children as a protection, for the enemy to see and fear God.

After his experience with the local herbalist, my dad said he confirmed my safety to those who had brought the negative report. He said he knew God had His protection around me. All the same, my dad was still concerned about my future, so he took me to see a prophetess. She was uneducated but had an incredible gift from God to reveal one's past, and to prophesy the future. When I sat in front of her, she revealed my experience in Nigeria. She said I would return to Nigeria again, and God's purpose would continue to be fulfilled in my life. She also confirmed my calling and encouraged me to study God's Word and remain faithful to Him.

While in Ghana, I attended a church called Gospel Light International. The senior pastor saw my passion for God and had a word with me. He led me to surrender my life publicly to the Lord Jesus Christ. I attended the baptism lessons and was then baptised by immersion in 1989. I started speaking in tongues as soon as I came out of the water, and since then I have continued to do so. As is written in the book of Jude 1:20, "But ye beloved, building up your most holy faith, praying in the Holy Ghost." The grace of God was upon me, and I preached the Gospel in Accra and in Cape Coast, Central Region, where I lived with my good friend Esther Arthur for about nine months. I helped to look after her new-born baby girl, while her husband was working abroad. After a year and half in Ghana, I felt the urge to return to the northern part of Nigeria for my hairdressing equipment and personal belongings. I told the senior pastor about it, and he prayed and helped me with some money for my journey. My family and friends also helped me with some money. I learnt that whatever one goes through in life, as one is obedient to God's calling, He provides whenever a need arises. God never fails. Prayer is the key.

Chapter 7

Visiting Prophet Charles Fynn

I returned safely to Lagos, knowing now that my steps were ordered by the Lord. Patiently waiting upon the Lord gave me a good understanding about things, and with time I learnt to know and trust the Lord more. He led me to a Bible school in Lagos. Thank God for the sound doctrine I received there, and the teaching to daily confess God's Word. As we read in Romans 1:17, "for therein is the righteousness of God revealed from faith to faith: as it is written, the just shall live by faith." The atmosphere at the school was always joyful. During praise and worship, we all danced and worshipped the LORD with all our might and strength.

I remember Prophet Charles Fynn, from the USA, who was invited to minister during a revival service. Everyone present at the meeting received a word of prophecy from God. As we lined up, I strongly felt the presence of God, and my body shook when it got to my turn. He spoke to me and said, "The Lord will send you with His Word to many, and the peace of God will be upon you, and what the enemy has thrust into your body, I cast out now in the name of the Lord Jesus. Be healed." I said a big Amen. The prophecy was simple and short, so I quickly wrote it down. Before the prophet gave me the message about the enemy thrusting something into my body, I was bleeding every day with severe abdominal pains. I had tried every pain killer I could buy from the pharmacy, but the pains had remained the same. Just like the woman with the issue of blood in the Bible, I went through this agony for over ten years.

After this prophecy, I reported my ordeal to my pastor at the school, and he prayed with me. He taught me to confess daily Isaiah fifty-three, verse five: "But he was wounded for our transgressions, he was bruised for our iniquities: the chastisement of our peace was upon him; and with his stripes we are healed." By God's grace, I had a successful fibroid operation when I finally returned to Ghana, and after that the bleeding stopped. You might be going through the same agony and pain. I want to encourage you that the Lord is your healer. The "how" and "when" is in His hands. If you come to Him by faith, He will heal you, and you will testify to His glory. Thank you, Lord Jesus.

Chapter 8

Five Years Of Training

I spent about a year in Lagos. I then found favour with the Alhaji, who gave me permission to collect my belongings. So, I went to the north for my things. As you can guess, all my belongings had been stolen. However, the Lord had a plan for me. I had returned to collect my things, but the Lord led me back to spend time studying His word and to understand the differences between Christianity and Islam. I attended the local Assemblies of God Church with all diligence. I studied Christian books, and I also read the English version of the Quran. I lived in the north for five years, and went through lack and difficulties, but the Lord supplied all my needs. I got to know the people well over time. The difference between the two religions became clear to me, as I spent time with the people.

To my simple knowledge, as I read the Bible, Christianity brings us the Gospel, the power of God unto salvation to all mankind. It is then up to the individual to accept the truth of God's Word. As is written in John's Gospel 3:16: "For God so loved the world that he gave his only begotten Son, that whosoever believeth in him should not perish, but have everlasting life." On the other hand, Islam seemed to me to be a religion which people accepted because they had been born into it, and not because of any personal experience of God. The less privileged Muslims depended on the leaders and the rich among them. Accommodation, farms and money were provided to help the needy. This was a good and kind act of giving, and no doubt the poor looked up to the rich. The Imams, leaders of the religion, taught the people about Allah and Mohammed as their prophet. The people in general were good and very kind, but no amount of preaching the Gospel changed them. I do believe I sowed good seed about the Gospel into their lives. In due time, the Lord hardened the heart of the Alhaji.

He became fed up with me living in his accommodation, and my daily preaching to the people in the area. He therefore arranged with the immigration authorities that I be repatriated to Ghana in 1995. Many years later, I received powerful testimonies of how some of the people I had witnessed to had given their lives to the Lord Jesus. To God be all the glory.

Chapter 9

Repatriation From Nigeria

After this second period of time living in Nigeria, I finally returned home to Ghana and was re-united with my family. My mum was so pleased to have me back to stay with her. I didn't know that she would pass away the following year. Months before she died, the Lord said to me, "Daughter it is now time for you to look for a mourning cloth." I kept asking the Lord, who is about to die, that I need to look for a mourning cloth? I did not get a reply till my mother passed away. After her death, the Lord gave me a reply in John's Gospel, chapter 12:24. "Verily, verily, I say unto you, except a corn of wheat fall into the ground and die, it abideth alone: but if it die, it bringeth forth much fruit." This helped me to accept that the Lord's will had been done, and His purposes would prevail. I was so close to my mother, and obviously her death did really affect me emotionally, because of loneliness, but the rest of my family stood with me. They were always there for me.

The same year that my mother passed away, a branch of Winners Chapel was opened in Ghana. It was called Word of Faith Bible Institute (WOFBI). I joined the Bible Institute and attended the basic Bible school in 1998. We were taught about God's salvation, for all who accepted Christ as their personal Saviour, including the benefits of living by faith according to the promises of God. For example, confessing God's promises aloud daily to express faith in God's Word. We also learnt how important it was to study the whole Bible. One must also spend quality time in fellowship with God and learn how to give generously. God gave His only begotten Son. We were taught that watching too many television programmes was one of the things to avoid, in order to stay closer to God. It was my sincere desire to know more of God, and to stay close to Him. I had just bought a new television, but my desire to know God caused me to give it to the Bible Institute to be sold and the money used for promoting the Gospel. What a privilege to be led on to the path of righteousness! Did not the Lord Jesus say we should put our treasures in heaven, where there are no moths and rust to destroy? Thank God for the Bible Institute. As I desired to do what was right and to draw closer to God, the Lord confirmed His calling upon my life by speaking to me through different people in various ways. If you are waiting on the Lord, you must be sensitive to the Holy Spirit, because God always speaks to us.

I recall the day I went to minister in a particular house. (I was moved by the Holy Spirit, during that period, to minister to people in their homes.) I told them about being born again through John's Gospel chapter three. We read and discussed the whole chapter. At the end I prayed for everyone, including a five-year-old girl who, after I had prayed for her, asked if she could pray for me. I was surprised because I was not expecting that. Apparently, she had arrived from the United States a week before my visit, and I was told she was prayerful and had the gift of prophecy, even at such a young age. I accepted her request and allowed her to pray for me. To my amusement, she opened her mouth and shouted, "Aunty Rita is a star! Amen." Then she went quiet. I replied, "Is that all you have to say?" She said yes. I thanked her, and I felt God spoke to me through her, to confirm how unique my calling was, and how I am fearfully and wonderfully made. (Psalm 139:14.)

Chapter 10
Somebody Robbed Me!

My love for God grew more and more as I spent time to seek His face. I travelled back to Lagos, in a long-distance taxi, to attend a Bible school for one month in 2001. It was a memorable journey of faith, because somebody robbed me. On the way we, the passengers, were told to cross a border by foot. During that time, unbeknown to me, somebody stole my purse containing all my money. I only took notice of it when I arrived in Lagos. But I'm glad to say that in my times of need, throughout the whole trip, the Lord worked miracles daily by providing accommodation, food and money for me. My predicament was announced on the opening day, when all of us attending the Leadership Bible School met together, and everyone present willingly gave me some help.

A Nigerian lady volunteered to take me in, and I then lived with her for some time. We became good friends. She provided money and food. We travelled to the Bible school together every day, in her car, which was fully air conditioned. One day, she told me that she was having some visitors, and this included her brother, who lived in Ghana. She knew I loved cooking and asked me to cook some Ghanaian food. When the visitors arrived, I was surprised to find that I knew her brother, from a church in Ghana. We realised that it was not by accident that we were now living together, but part of God's plan. When we finished the course she didn't want me to leave, so I stayed with her for another two months before I returned to Ghana. I also visited the Alhaji and told him that my purse had been stolen, after my new friend encouraged me to do so. She said to trust God, and He would give me favour. And truly, God did give me favour when the Alhaji gave me 3,000 naira! I gave my friend 1000 naira, to thank her for all her help. When I returned to Ghana, I brought back so much money, despite my purse having been stolen.

Chapter 11
Hastening Into The Wrong Marriage

In the year 2002, I became a victim of pressure to marry. I was forty-four years old. All my siblings were married and had children. I was the eldest among my three sisters and was still single. (I mention earlier in my book that I was my father's only daughter. My two sisters are half-sisters, the daughters of my mum. I also have an older half-brother, who lives in the UK.) My friends did not understand the fact that God had called me for a purpose. I had also forgotten the prophecy about the noble man I received from the LORD while I was in Celestia Church of Christ in 1985. The enemy of my soul, Satan, took advantage of my situation to avert the plan of God for my life. Because of this, my friends started to pressurise me to get married. Whenever I visited them, they said things like "Did you not read in the Bible that no one will marry in heaven?" "You are a beautiful woman, if you wait till you are old, nobody will marry you." "You are wasting your beauty." "Get married before it is too late!" "Your late mother married your dad and gave birth to you. You also get married and give birth to children." These words made me feel really guilty, as if I had committed a crime by being single. Many a time, we all succumb to moments of pressure in various ways. If I knew then what I know now, I would have waited patiently on the Lord for the right person in God's time.

My younger sister introduced me to a Christian man called Dan* from a foreign country. The only way we could get to know each other was by communicating on the internet and speaking on the phone. He came to Ghana after six months and we got engaged; traditionally we were married. We then proceeded to sign the official registry. We lived in my youngest sister's house. We then started

---

* This name has been changed.

attending a local church. It was a Pentecostal church close to our home. I entered into this relationship as a born-again child of God, but without inquiring from the Lord if that was His will for me. You can imagine how everything happened so quickly. Dan started having an affair with our house help. For some reason, Dan started having his meals before I returned from work. He stayed at home because he was looking for work at that time. When I asked him why he no longer waited for me, he said it was because he felt too hungry to wait. Later, I received information from a neighbour, who lived opposite us, that she watched Dan and the house help eat together, and even saw Dan fondle her. From then on, I noticed how they were truly fond of each other. I did not waste any more time but quickly sent her away. Dan got so angry because I sent her away. He soon started picking quarrels with me, till it came to a point that we were not talking to each other at home.

I acknowledged I had missed my way with the Lord. I humbled myself and pleaded with Dan for us to seek help from the Lord through prayer and fasting, but he refused and said he would have nothing to do with me. So, I fasted and prayed for twenty-one days, eating only in the evenings. During this difficult period, I privately told the senior pastor of the church about my predicament and asked for his advice. He encouraged me to put my trust in God. He then called Dan and heard his side of the matter. The pastor did his best to bring us together, but it was too late. However, his word of encouragement brought hope to me, as I did not know how to get out of this mess. I sincerely believed it was only God who could bring me out of my trouble.

At this point, I would like to share with you what I did after my prayer and fasting. I sowed a seed in the House of God, and some years later God gave me a testimony to share with many and include in this book. (Genesis 8:22, "While the earth remaineth, seedtime and harvest, and cold and heat, and summer and winter, and day and night shall not cease.") Our church needed funds and materials to build a wall around the property. I thought I had a duty to put God's House first. I went and withdrew all my savings and closed my account. I then bought twenty-one bags of cement and gave the remaining money as a seed offering to the House of God. When the senior pastor learnt of what I had done, I remember him asking me, "Did you really close your bank account?" I replied, "Yes, Pastor." He then prayed and pronounced blessings upon me with all his heart. Nobody told me to do this, and I do not approve of people being pressurised to make offerings or approve of the "prosperity Gospel" that has taken root in many places. We are to give to help others, and obey God when He prompts us, not in response to manipulation, or with the expectation that we will become rich.

Three months after the house help left, Dan and I started discussing divorce, which we thought could be the best solution. It was, as the saying goes, "Quick to get in, quick to get out", after just over a year. By this time there was nothing else that we could do, though I continued to hope and trust in the Lord. My sister had meant well for me concerning this marriage, but as a born-again child of God, had it really been the plan of God for me?

In January 2004, news of the sudden death of my younger brother's wife, who lived in London, reached my family in Ghana. We were all shocked. Our consolation, despite our grief, was that she was truly a born-again child of God. She left behind three children, Kwame, Mama and Nanaaba, the youngest, named after me. I was invited to attend her funeral. To give some background information, two years before my younger sister introduced me to Dan, I had an invitation from a cousin to travel to the USA. After spending a lot of money on the visa application and interview, I was refused a visa to travel. The reason for the refusal was that I had nothing to prove that, if I was given a visa, I would return. As I had no husband, children or property in Ghana, the American embassy suspected that I would stay permanently. I was therefore pleased when I received the invitation to travel to London.

While I was thanking God for sending me an invitation to travel, Dan was aggrieved. My daddy suggested he should go back to his country and join me later to attend the funeral. His response to this suggestion was that it was impossible for him to travel, because he was bankrupt in his own country and therefore could not return there for the next five years. All that he had covered up was uncovered, because of my sudden need to travel abroad.

At that time, one of my sisters dreamt that Dan had a fierce argument with me and tore up all my travel documents, including my passport. As soon as I got this information from my sister, I took all my important documents and gave them to my elder brother for safe keeping. I then prayed and fasted for three days, asking God to help me. Dan didn't know about my sister's dream. By then he was working with a friend, who had a business in Ghana. He pretended he was ill and stayed at home. For three days, he searched through my suitcases for my documents and found nothing. He did not ask me anything and I also kept the peace. I had applied for my UK visa and had been given a date for my interview.

On the morning of my interview, Dan was so angry that he refused to accompany me. With prayers, hope and faith in God, I went to the British High Commission alone and was successful. The interview went smoothly and was short. The only question the lady asked was "Where is your husband?" "He is at home," I replied, with a smile on my face. She smiled back and said I should go home and return for my visa in the afternoon. When I returned to collect my passport containing the visa, I was full of joy. I went straight to my elder brother and gave my passport to him. As soon as I got back home and Dan found out I had given my passport to my brother, he reacted by speaking ungodly words against me and my family. He tore into pieces all our photographs, even breaking the frames. He also took my engagement Bible, secretly, while searching through my suitcases. I refused to answer him a word. For two weeks I did my best to keep the peace, and I prayed to God to help me.

Chapter 12

Problem With My Passport

Fortunately, I was able to buy a three month return promotional ticket to London. The funeral of my sister-in-law was on the 20th February 2004, and I was due to travel on the 18th February. I was accompanied by Dan to the airport. There was a long queue at the check-in counter. When it got to my turn, the immigration officer, after glancing through my passport, asked me to stand aside. My first two sentences were, "Oh no, not again" and "What have I done?" Then I said a prayer: "Dear Lord, please help me and let your will be done. Amen."

Some minutes after I prayed, the immigration officer told me that he was sorry, but I would not be travelling that day. I asked him why. Firstly, he mentioned that the profession written in my passport was prophetess. He also said that they were not certain that the British embassy had issued me with the visa. He led me to the chief immigration officer, who said my passport should be taken back to the British Embassy the following morning for confirmation of its validity. I tried my best to refute the accusation that my visa was not genuine, but it was too late. As I talked to them, I saw the plane take off.

Dan was very happy that I was unable to travel. He even said that God had prevented me from travelling. I did not understand why I was in such a predicament. During the night, I prayed to God to intervene on my behalf, to prove to men that He had called me as a prophetess, to be used for His Kingdom, and also to make a way for me where there seemed to be no way. (When I had returned from Nigeria, my passport had been overdue for renewal. I had not foreseen any problem putting "Prophetess" as my profession in my passport. I was all out for God and had no plan B for my life. However, I do understand now that putting that profession in my passport would seem very strange to a lot of people and could have a negative impact getting through immigration checks!) I asked the Lord if it was His will for me to travel the following day. I prayed till the early hours of the morning and slept for just two hours. I woke up with excitement within me, that come what may I would fly that day, 19th February 2004.

At twelve midday, I received a phone call from the British Embassy in Ghana. The lady caller told me that my passport had been confirmed and given back to the Ghanaian immigration authorities. I should therefore go and collect it and continue my journey. I offered praise and thanksgiving to God for my vindication. I want to comment here that whatever one's calling, it will be questioned one day. I believe that when God calls men, He is able to vindicate those that He has called when they are questioned.

Dan was not at home, so I called my elder brother, who went with me to collect my passport. He and his wife were keen to help me to travel, to enable me to represent them at the funeral. Because I had missed my flight, the airline told me that my money was not refundable. Though they would allow me to travel on another promotional flight, in three weeks' time. Fortunately, my elder brother's wife, Mrs Ellen Hagan, knew the manageress of the airline, so she spoke on my behalf and my ticket money was given back to me. I saw the intervention of God, because I had closed my bank account and could not afford a full British Airways ticket. I saw God helping me through my brother and his wife, as they added more money to my refund. They immediately bought me a year's return British Airways ticket to travel that day. I repaid them later. Time did not allow me to go home for my suitcase, so I called Dan and he agreed to bring it to the airport. Dan was amazed that everything had changed so quickly and I was now able to travel. He then suddenly changed towards me, and revealed his true intentions, as he pleaded with me to send him seventy pounds every week. I did not answer him a word, and that was the last time I ever saw his face.

(I was not in a position to send Dan any money, when I arrived in London, therefore he refused to talk to me. He sent me an email which stated that, whether I liked it or not, he had divorced me. I later received information from the church that he had suffered serious financial hardship. Because of that, he had participated in the fasting and praying that took place over twenty-one days. His family later sent him a ticket, and he returned to his own country.)

When I was finally checked in by the airline, I felt so happy. Imagine how grateful and thankful I was, first to God, and then to my elder brother and his wife. With a joyful heart, I entered the plane and thanked God for making it possible for me to travel. I arrived safely, just in time for the burial of my sister-in-law. The undertakers were ready on the road in front of the house, waiting for the family to follow them. I quickly changed my clothes and went with the family to the cemetery. After the burial, I thought about this new chapter, and all the uncertainty that lay ahead of me.

My bereaved brother needed help to care for his children. My brother's mother-in-law, who lived with them, had applied for indefinite stay to help, but the authorities had turned her application down. I had only a six months visa, but I was independent and had no children, so my family thought I was the right person for this purpose. I realised that God had turned things around for me to remain in the UK. It took the grace of God for the children to come to terms with the loss of their mother. It was not easy for them to accept me in the beginning, although I was their dad's big sister. As their auntie, I daily took everything to the Lord in prayer, confessing blessings over them and anointing their beds. I believed that one day all would end well, and they would thank God for bringing me to help them during their bereavement.

As for me, given my predicament back home, I did not take it lightly that I should be living in London. I felt relieved, and my heart was filled with gratitude to God. I asked the Lord for direction over which church I should attend. I did not want to make any more mistakes over my precious life. This was a new opportunity that the Lord had given me. One day Sister Serwah, a family friend, dropped an invitation from her church through the letterbox. My brother commented that he did not need an invitation from any church, and even joked that it might be for me. There was no Winners Chapel around the area yet, and since I did not know exactly which church I should attend, I decided to go and see things for myself.

It was in April 2004 that I first visited the Living Springs International Church. After I attended that first family service, I felt it was the right church for me. I became a full member after attending all their services for about a year. I was so happy that I had found a church where I could always praise and dance unto the Lord. Dancing before the Lord was something I had learnt at Winners Chapel. I also confided in my pastor and told him about my situation with Dan in Ghana. He prayed with me to break the spiritual ties with Dan. I followed that up by burying my engagement ring. I desired a new ring someday. After that, I felt a burden was lifted from my shoulders. I then shared the testimony of my deliverance to many. Things also gradually began to settle down at home, for me and my new family.

My brother introduced me to his lawyer, who sent my application for an indefinite stay to the Home Office. Sadly, when the reply came after a year, I was refused my visa to remain, because the lawyer made a mistake with my application. He did not clarify to the Home Office that my brother had his own accommodation, and therefore I was not going to be a burden on public funds. He then made an appeal on my behalf, on the grounds that my bereaved nieces had become used to my presence and needed my continued help. They were pleased to live with me, rather than having to rely on support from social services. Indeed, they wrote a personal appeal to support my claim. In addition, the lawyer now sent the correct information, proving that my brother was a homeowner.

My brother and his children gradually accepted their situation and moved on. I continued daily in prayer for their salvation and made every effort to make them happy. The Lord answered my prayers and brought comfort to them. Mama and Nanaaba got born again, by surrendering their life to the Lord Jesus, to the glory of God. I didn't realise that the Lord would answer so quickly. It was a great joy on that beautiful Sunday in church, (at the Triumphant Global Ministry) when I witnessed them both sharing the testimony of their faith in Christ.

Chapter 13

Immigration Problems

I soon started having problems with immigration, because my appeal to the Home Office was refused. I then made my final appeal to a higher court. My brother's lawyer had told me to see to it myself, as he didn't expect me to succeed. I quickly decided it was beyond my power to solve the issue, so I handed it over to the Lord. One Sunday, I took a seed offering and all my documents, including my passport, to the church, to surrender it all to the Lord for His help. When I arrived, there was no one there except the cleaner who opened the door. So, I went and knelt before the altar and poured out my heart to God.

During the praise and worship time, I gave the Lord a very good dance with all my heart and strength which brought a lot of laughter and joy to the church. Though no one knew why I danced. Immediately after the praise and worship, the coordinator of the service took the microphone and said, "There is someone here who is taking his or her papers to the Home Office, to appeal for indefinite stay, and the Lord says He will get you your stay." Hearing that, I ran up to the altar, knelt down and worshipped the Lord, giving Him thanks with all my heart. This word from God had come forth with grace and power, and I believed it. I held on to Psalm twenty-four, verse one: "The earth is the LORD'S, and the fullness thereof; the world, and they that dwell therein." Another scripture that encouraged me to keep trusting in the Lord was the book of Joshua chapter one, verse three: "Every place that the sole of your foot shall tread upon, that have I given unto you as I said unto Moses." You may argue that the promise was made to the children of Israel. Yes, but I also felt God was speaking to me, as I know who I am in Christ. I am a child of God, living a life of favour. God's Word gave me the strength, and hope, to wait upon the Lord.

After the service, I took all my documents and showed them to Brother Eugene, the coordinator. He prayed with me that God would bring His word to pass in my life. I also thanked him for being sensitive to the Holy Spirit and speaking God's Word of promise to meet my need. That day, I went home and told my brother Atta how God had spoken to me concerning my stay, and that because I believed I did not need any solicitor but would speak for myself in court. However, my brother advised me that in the United Kingdom one cannot go to court concerning immigration issues without a solicitor. He told me to go to the Citizen's Advice Bureau. I did not want any arguments with my brother, so I went for the service which was free. I was given a solicitor to help me with my situation and eventually to defend me in court. In May 2005, I started attending Ms Harriet Harman's surgery in Camberwell, as she was my local MP. The surgery helped with my correspondence with the Home Office. The solicitor from the Citizen's Advice Bureau, and the staff of my MP, worked together to prepare me for court.

The date of the court hearing was the 25th September 2005. Early in the morning, around 8.00am, the solicitor called, and said he had a severe headache and would not be able to attend. He advised me to go, but he said the court magistrate would surely adjourn the case. My brother went with me. My experience in the court that day is something I will never forget. There were about four cases before mine, and we waited for several hours. Finally, we were called into the court room. When the magistrate was informed that my solicitor had been taken ill, we were thinking he would adjourn the case. However, to our surprise, he decided to continue. I had requested for a Ghanaian interpreter, to help me to understand, and also to give me time to think carefully before I answered the magistrate. All together there were five of us: the magistrate, immigration officer, the interpreter, my brother Atta, and myself. The immigration officer was determined that I be sent home immediately, because I had overstayed my visa, but God intervened on my behalf. The magistrate put questions to me and my brother. The room was tense. The immigration officer kept saying I had overstayed my visa. He even said that his own mother had died when he was ten years old, and nobody had come to look after him. At this point I was praying silently in tongues. (Praying in the Holy Spirit.) We were in the room for over forty-five minutes, and I heard a voice saying to me, "The earth is the Lord's, and the fullness thereof, the world and they that dwell in it." (Psalm 24:1) Another voice said, "Today you are returning back home. You have overstayed!"

Eventually, the court magistrate said, "Ms. Hagan, looking through your passport, the occupation recorded is prophetess. Now tell me, what do you do? Do you read palms or what? Explain yourself." I was lost for words, and said to myself, "Oh, my passport and my profession again! Dear Lord, help me!" But I also quickly remembered the Lord's words, "For whosoever shall be ashamed of me and of my words, of him shall the Son of Man be ashamed" (Luke 9:26). At that moment, I encouraged myself and lifted up my voice with boldness and said, "My lord, I am an evangelist, I preach the Gospel of our Lord Jesus Christ!" As soon as I mentioned the Lord's name, there was an amazing quietness and sense of God's presence in the room. We all bowed our heads, including the magistrate. It was awesome, and a moment I cannot fully explain. I looked straight at the magistrate, and he looked puzzled, scratching his head. He replied by asking me, "Which church do you attend?" "Living Springs International Church", I replied. He said, "So you bring men to God?" I replied, "Yes, my lord."

(Food for thought: I believe that when the magistrate took my passport and saw my profession, he may have felt: "This is evidence that I can use to challenge this woman and may be grounds to send her back home. In the UK, able workers are given permits to remain, and pay taxes, for the good of the country. What benefit is this woman bringing to the UK?" But God had a plan and a purpose for me. We are all different in God's eyes, with different callings. God rules in the affairs of men, and He has the final say!)

In response to my words, he then recommended that I be given leave to remain, on compassionate grounds, for another year. He acknowledged that my nieces had grown attached to me, and that I was a great help to them, as my brother had made clear. He suggested that I get letters from various organizations, such as my church, social services, and my niece's doctor, and then ask my solicitor to use these in support of my case. The immigration officer apologised for being harsh with me, adding that he was only doing his job. The court was asked to rise, and it was all over.

What a miracle! God, my Father, had intervened, and touched the heart of the magistrate, so that His purpose for me in this land would be fulfilled. "It is of the LORD'S mercies that we are not consumed, because his compassions fail not." (Lamentation 3:22) "Who is he that saith, and it cometh to pass, when the Lord commandeth it not." (Lamentation 3:37) These were the scriptures that came into my mind and helped me to be confident in the Lord God. This was a moment of my destiny, determined by God rather than man. If God had not come through for me, where would I be today?

My solicitor contacted me after recovering from his severe headache. Because he had been unable to attend the court, he felt obliged to help me send my papers to the Home Office. I collected letters of support to submit with my new application. I gave them to my solicitor, who sent them, with a covering letter, to the Home Office by the end of October 2005.

Chapter 14
Bible College

My work with an agency came to an end, because the management of the school decided to employ me directly, on a full-time basis, but I was asked to bring my residence permit to the school and could not do so, as I had not yet heard from the Home Office. I rested at home for a month, and then decided to look for another job. Fortunately, I found a cleaning company who urgently needed workers. The work was outside London, and we were to clean primary schools. I loved cleaning, so I was happy to go for it.

After nine months of travelling outside London to clean, I changed my mind about the cleaning work. I felt I needed to attend a Bible College to "study to show myself approved unto God, a workman that needed not to be ashamed, rightly dividing the word of truth." (2 Timothy 2:15). While at work, I daily spoke positive words about the Bible College and my future. I confessed I did not come to London to clean all my life, therefore something miraculous must happen for me to attend the Bible College. I put the power of the tongue into practice. I rejoiced while lifting up the hoover from one classroom to another. My daily song was: "Lord lift me up to where I belong." I had not heard from the Home Office, but my solicitor assured me that no news was good news. With his assurance, I believed my indefinite stay was in the post, so that I could attend a Bible College.

At the end of May 2006, we had a programme in our church, and the founder, Pastor Frank Ofosu-Appiah, was invited from Atlanta, Georgia. He taught us on the subject of stewardship in the body of Christ. While he was teaching us, I felt the need for direction from God about which Bible College to attend. I knew that London was vast, and I didn't know exactly where to go. I decided therefore to sow seed into the founder's life and ask him to stand in a prayer of agreement with me. After the meeting, I gave him the seed, and told him of my desire to attend a Bible college and my need for God's direction. His reply was: "Daughter of Zion, go in faith, and receive direction from God." I replied "Amen." That same week, the cleaning company told me my contract had ended. I was asked to stay at home till I heard from them.

In the first week of August, I went to my pastor, and asked him if there were any Bible Colleges that he could recommend. He gave me a brochure for South London Christian College, which he said the church had just received. He told me to go and read through, and if I liked it, he would gladly help with my application. I was pleased with everything about the college, especially the three days attendance in a week, from Tuesday to Thursday. Since I had not heard from the cleaning company, I felt there was an opportunity for me to attend the Bible college. I applied, with faith in God, and even asked for a scholarship. I needed two references, so my pastor and a church member, Minister Solomon, gave me references which I posted by recorded delivery. I received a reply after a week and went for an interview, which I passed. I enrolled as a student at the college, with a half scholarship, even though I had still not heard from the Home Office. I thought this could only be the favour of God.

(By this time, my brother and his children had recovered from their bereavement and were coping better. That encouraged me to attend the Bible college. I was introduced to a married couple in our church, who needed a helping hand with their two children, Awura and Papa. I moved in to help care for their children. After six months of living together, the family saw the need for a full-time helper, so I needed to move on again, as I was busy with the Bible school. After that, I lived in various places but returned to live with my brother at times, if I had nowhere else to go, and especially if my brother was away in Ghana and needed someone to look after his house. Naanaba and Mama, my nieces, were older then, and away in boarding school much of the time.)

The Lord ordered my steps and helped me to attend South London Christian College in September 2006. A good deed worth sharing with you concerning the college was done by Bishop Frank Ofosu-Appiah, the founder of our church, Living Springs International. (I mentioned before how I sowed a seed into his life, while seeking direction from God.) He was on the board of directors of the college, and voluntarily served for a year without pay. I was touched by this benevolent deed of giving, and I was glad I sowed into his life after hearing this testimony about him. I learnt that whatever good deed you sow, you will also reap someday.

I attended the college for a year, and still had no reply from the Home Office. The authorities of the college asked me to bring my residence permit. I wrote to inform the Home Office, through my local MP's surgery, of my current circumstances. The Home Office replied, giving me 28 days' notice to leave the UK, and return with a student visa to attend the Bible College. When I read the letter, my first comment was: "Satan, you are a liar! The Lord my God has already said He will get me my stay." I thought in my heart, whose report should I believe? (Isaiah 53:1) This challenge came like a great storm. Like Hezekiah in the book of Isaiah 38:1-3, I placed the letter before the Lord in prayer, and I reminded Him of the word He gave me from the pulpit in Living Springs. I remember I took the letter to my family friend, Sister Cynthia Osei, and we prayed earnestly and asked God to deliver me from my present trouble. She then gave me a word from the Lord, "Confirmation", to confirm that surely the issue of my stay in the UK was settled. Turning the clock backwards, I thought I had made a mistake, when I wrote to the Home Office of my change in circumstances. Sometimes, we all regret our past mistakes, and the decisions we have taken. However, I encourage you to be strong and not to be afraid of the challenges of life, they are not permanent. But always remember to take it to the Lord in prayer and trust Him. It could be a test of your faith in Christ.

I became even more concerned about my situation, when I took the letter to show the principal of the college. Being in a Bible college, I was confident that my principal would pray and encourage me in my faith in God. When he read the letter, his immediate response was, "If the Home Office said you should return home for a student visa, then that is the law of this country." He therefore advised me to do so. I am ever grateful to my principal. He did all he could to help me, but remember, God said we should not put our trust in man. To the glory of God, as it is written in Romans 8:28, "And we know that all things work together for good to them that love God, to them who are the called according to his purpose." I testify that the Lord helped me through my time at college. I did not return home, but completed a diploma in Ministerial Studies, by His grace. The course included Theology, Greek, Old and New Testament Survey, New Creation Studies, Counselling, Psychology, Foundational Doctrines, Ecclesiology, Pentecostal Theology, Blood Covenant, Doctrine of God and Trinity, Christian Ethics, Pastoral Epistles and Hermeneutics. I thank God for giving me the grace to study His Word.

Chapter 15
Home Calling Of My Dearest Dad

The happy days of my childhood with my dad had been cut short. For some inexplicable reason, my dad drove me out of our family home. Though I begged him not to send me away, he refused. So, I left him and lived with my mum. That was the main reason why I travelled at a young age, to live and work in Nigeria. It is only now that I can say it may have been the plan of God for me to travel to Nigeria. When I gave my life to the Lord Jesus as my Lord and Saviour, I received the grace to forgive my dad. God brought us together in London during the funeral of my late sister-in-law. After the burial, dad had a teeth transplant, which made him stay longer than he had originally planned. For three months, I cooked his meals and cared for him. It was a sweet reunion and he blessed me before he returned to Ghana. It was the last time I saw his face.

In December 2007, during my time at Bible school, I received an appeal form from the Home Office. My MP had written to the Home Office asking them to reconsider my case, because of the long delays in responding to my letters. My MP pleaded that I should be granted leave to remain in the UK, on compassionate grounds. With the help of my solicitor, my appeal form was filled in, and sent to the Home Office on the 13th December. On that same day, I called my dad in Ghana and told him the good news. I promised that I would come to Ghana as soon as I received my leave to remain. He replied saying, "Nanaaba, don't worry, trust only in the Lord whom you serve, for I know the Lord will bless you with your stay and a good husband."

On the 26th December, I called my dad to wish him merry Christmas and a happy new year, though he did not live to see it. I received a phone call from my brother, early in the morning on the 31st December, and he told me that my Dad had gone to be with the Lord. The shocking thing about my dad's death, was that it came just four days after I had spoken to him. According to my brother, Dad fell down the stairs and bruised his hernia wound. (He had had a successful operation in the first week of November.) Dad was rushed to the hospital, and by the third day he looked so well that everyone who visited him thought he was coming home soon. However, on the fourth day he died in his sleep, at the age of eighty-one years old. It was a great blessing for us his children for Dad to die peacefully.

My dad had surrendered his life to Christ. I give thanks to God that he was saved before he died. After his death, I prayed to God desiring to see him in my dreams, and God granted my desire. Seven days after he passed away, I dreamt he was sitting on a bed next to me, with a bit of a gap between us. He was wearing a white singlet and shorts, clothes which I knew very well. He was full of smiles and laughter, and I was also laughing. I started a conversation: "Daddy so you are not dead, and I was told you are dead." He replied, "Don't mind them, if I was dead, would I be talking to you?" "Oh," I commented, "Why should I be told a lie?" He said, "My daughter, Nanaaba, serve your God well. Be kind and do good to all the people you come across, and don't worry about the will I left behind. Everything will be alright with you." Suddenly I realised that we were walking outside. I lifted up my eyes and I saw two people coming towards us. It was a bit dark, and I tried to see who they were. When I turned again to talk to my dad, he was not with me. I got up and sat on my bed, and I acknowledged it was a dream. I quickly wrote down the conversation and started praising and thanking God for a wonderful dream of my dad. I was now sure he was gone, and I felt so lonely. I was the only one among my brothers and sisters who was not married or settled in life. Dad was buried on the 26th January 2008. Sadly, I was unable to travel because my appeal to the Home Office had not been answered. It was a hard time for me, with many afflictions to bear. I cried to God to help me and to show me what to do next.

Chapter 16
Answer To My Cry

Some days after my dad's burial, out of stress and uncertainty, I knelt before God, as naked as the day that I came into this world and cried earnestly to Him. Sometimes we need to go deep to reach out to God. He is a merciful Father. The Lord answered my cry and turned my life around. This is how it happened. Prophet Ron and Prophetess Jane Jolliff from Ohio, USA, were invited by Dr Curdell McLeod, to minister in South London Christian College. The principal of the college sent a text message, inviting me to a prophetic meeting on the 3rd February 2008. His specific words were: "If I were you, I would come and hear from the prophets." I was so surprised when I read the text that I called the principal. I asked him how he knew about my desperate need to hear from God. His reply was, "Just come empty and you will be filled." I was more than willing to hear from the prophets. On that Sunday, I went to Living Springs for praise and worship, before going to the prophetic meeting. I arrived at the time the sermon was being preached by Prophet Ron. I sat in the back row and prayed quietly saying, "Father in heaven, please talk to your daughter, please don't fail me." As soon as I finished praying, the prophet ended the sermon and he said they needed to minister to individuals. My heart was panting after God, longing for Him to speak to me. I was the fourth person to be called. The prophecy confirmed my calling to minister God's Word to many. Thankfully, I was provided with a DVD video recording after the service.

These are the words of the prophet spoken to me that day. He asked my name and said, "Lord, we thank you for Claudia. The Lord says He has put a merry heart in you, my daughter. The Lord says you have a heart of joy! I hear the Lord saying He is going to use you to minister to many people. The Lord says because you have been beaten up, downtrodden and wounded. The Lord says: 'I am going to take you into a higher place. I have given you creativity. There is creativity all over you. I have given you the arts to flow all over you. Even in the dance and even in the song, the song of the Lord will flow out of you.' The Lord says: 'Daughter get ready, get ready, get ready.' The Lord says the release is coming. The Lord says, 'I have broken all small things and I am going to bring on something new.' And so the Lord says, 'Daughter, the day of breaking through is now, so rise up, oh daughter of Zion.' The Lord says: 'I am even putting in you a heart of an intercessor. Prophetic intercession will be a part of you: even now you are in the place, allow Him to raise you up slowly. I will bring adjustments. I will make a way where there seems to be no way. There have been situations that you have had to walk out of, that have hurt you, but allow that to be a teaching thing. I am going to cause you to be raised up again even in the proper season and at the proper time,' says the Lord. We release that to her. We thank you Lord Jesus, we release that to her right now in the name of the Lord Jesus. Amen."

I received fresh anointing with hope and strength, especially a gift of joy in the Holy Ghost. I love the Lord Jesus so much, and truly He is the rewarder of those who diligently seek Him. (Hebrews 11:6). After the encounter with the prophets, I was so thankful to God, who had immediately given an answer to my cry. I believed what the prophet said, so I confessed the words daily and trusted God to bring them to pass.

On Good Friday, in April 2008, I was invited to an all-night prayer meeting, at the church connected to the college. The principal, Dr Femi, was ministering. He said, by revelation, that God wanted those willing to evangelise the lost to come forward, for him to anoint them with oil. I was the only one to run forward. As he took the anointing oil, he said the Lord was giving me a new name, Joy. I shouted "Amen." He then anointed me with the oil, and I fell under the power of God. Truly the anointing breaks the yoke. (Isaiah 10:27) The experience was awesome. From that day onwards, I designed my own Gospel tracts for publication, and started preaching to people in Peckham and wherever I went. I also evangelised on buses and trains as I travelled around London, speaking one to one to those who were willing to listen. God gave me wisdom about whom to talk to. What a joy and a blessing to work in God's Kingdom!

In March 2009, Prophet Ron and Prophetess Jane Jollif came again. I invited two friends, Mrs Victoria Bonsu and Sister Praise, to come and hear from God. They came with excitement, after hearing my testimony, and they also prayed that the Lord would speak to them. The ministration of the prophets to them was accurate. The Lord indeed spoke to meet their need. I was not expecting the prophet to call me forward that day, but God had a surprise for me. I was the first to be called. This time it was a short prophecy, which someone wrote down for me. This is what he said: "Daughter, I have called you, and even now you are in the process of preparation. I am going to use you greatly, and now I have even anointed you with such anointing as Prophetess Deborah in the Bible. Satan and men will try to stop you from keeping focus, but I, the Lord, will uphold you, and keep you till you fulfil your calling. You will dance in my House, before my Presence, with a new song flowing in your mouth. I, the Lord, will hasten my word to perform it." It was a confirmation of the prophecy I received in 2008. My two friends and I were blessed by the accuracy of the prophecies. After the service, we had a chat with the Jollifs, and I realised they did not remember me. I told them I had received a similar prophecy when they came before. Praise the Lord!

You may ask why I am writing so much about these prophets. Well, first of all, as a prophetess by the calling of God, I promote the ministry of God's true senior prophets. Secondly, I cried earnestly to God to speak to me, and He sent His prophets who told me all that I went through and suffered while I was in Nigeria. An accurate word of prophecy can have a powerful impact on a person's life. A biblical example is the testimony of the woman of Samaria.

"Come, see a man which told me all things that ever I did: is not this the Christ?" (John 4:29) I went through a very long period of afflictions for twenty-seven years. The Lord did speak to me in different ways, however the one which turned my life around for excellence was hearing from the prophets. That made a significant difference in my life. I experienced the positive impact of prophecy, held fast to what I received from the Lord, and prayed with positive confession till it came to pass. 2 Chronicles 20:20 confirms what I am trying to explain. "Believe in the LORD your God, so shall ye be established: believe his prophets, so shall ye prosper." When the prophet spoke to me, it was a confirmation of what I knew about myself, but it also gave me revelation about my future. The Lord turned my mourning to dancing. Who wants afflictions all the time? The timely prophecy I received increased my faith and hope in God. If the prophets had not spoken to me, I may not have written this book of hope in Christ.

You can also trust God, whatever your circumstance, to bring you a timely word. The Almighty God sends angels, prophets, and people into our lives, to help us with the things only He can bring to pass. Please make every effort to sow seed by giving to the prophets and men of God, who God sends to you. Don't turn them away, and miss the opportunity God may be giving you, because of some bad experiences in the past with fake or dubious people. Receive and hear from them, test their spirit to see if they are from God, as true ministry could lead to a breakthrough in your life.

Chapter 17

Memorable Piece Of Advice.

It is always good to read God's Word; you receive wisdom and understanding, and it makes you live your life in a way that is pleasing to the Lord. The word of God written in Proverbs 19:14 says: "A prudent wife is from the LORD." That particular verse opened my eyes, and I made up my mind to wait on the Lord for a good husband. Given what I had experienced before, after entering into a hasty marriage, I did everything I could to find out more about any man who came into my life. Pastor Bossman, who was once my pastor, gave me some very good advice worth sharing with you. His advice was powerful and thoughtful. He said, as a single woman waiting on the Lord for a good husband, I was to be like an 'Akatasia', a Fanti word from Ghana meaning a covered young woman. A woman kept her honour, he continued, when the right man married her before sharing a bed with her. (Hebrews 13:4, "Marriage is honourable in all, and the bed undefiled: but whoremongers and adulterers God will judge.")

Pastor Bossman drew my attention to the literal meaning of Akatasia: a covered young woman who dresses properly, without exposing her body to attract men, but waits for "Mr. Right" to honour her in marriage. I was overwhelmed to hear that, for I had never thought of it in that manner. He further explained that if a woman allows any man to sleep with her before marriage, given the fact that he had not committed himself to the relationship, or paid any dowry, he could decide not to marry her. If that happens, it is heart-breaking and brings dishonour with daily regrets. He was very straight with me, as he said he was also a man, and some men would do anything to satisfy their lust. This piece of advice helped me to overcome all the temptations that came my way.

My pastor stood with me in prayer and told me to bring to him any man who came into my life. I took two men who came my way and, with his help, we found out that they were fake. Singles and beautiful virgins in Christ, honour God with your bodies, open your eyes wide, and remember the enemy is roaring like a lion, seeking whom he may devour. The things we go through in life give us the experience needed to advise others, so that they can take precautions.

I received a strange call from a man, who told me that God had sent him to enable me to obtain my indefinite stay. He said he would marry me. I had met this man early one morning, while I was evangelising on a bus. He took my phone number and encouraged me to continue spreading the Gospel. Later that day, I knelt down in prayer and cried to God, with tears running down my face. I asked God to remember me from His throne of mercy, concerning my immigration situation. When I finished praying, the man I met earlier called me. As soon as I answered the phone, he said I should stop crying, God had told him to help me. He said he was the one God had prepared for me to marry, as soon as possible, so that I could get my papers. I was short of words and amazed. I wondered how he knew that I was crying, asking God to help me. Nevertheless, as I am writing now, I can tell you in the mighty name of the Lord Jesus, that it was the devil himself who sent his agent. He came like an angel of light. Having learnt from my previous experiences, I was confident to deal with him myself. I fasted and prayed about what he said and tested his spirit by inviting him to church. He gave many excuses and failed to come. I thought if God had sent him, he would love to come to church with me. God exposed him, as he argued with me concerning God's Word, to satisfy his lust. Instead, he invited me to a five-star hotel in London. However, because I knew the truth in the Word of God concerning marriage, I overcame him, and he quickly disappeared.

That was not the end. Seven other men from the enemy's camp also came and tried to take advantage of me. The Lord shielded me under His wings, until Mr Right came into my life. The Bible makes clear that the Christian woman should marry a Christian husband and wait until marriage for sexual intimacy. We are not to be "unequally yoked", so that our own faith is not undermined by an unbelieving spouse, taking us away from the things of God. If we make this mistake God is still merciful, and will help us as we repent, but it will have negative consequences in our lives. I learnt the hard way to wait on God for a husband, having suffered from my own mistake, in rushing into an unwise relationship. That is why it is on my heart to warn others. Why did I go through all these trials and temptations? It is because the devil knew of the word of promise I had received from the Lord, in 1985 in Nigeria. That was a prophecy that a noble man would kneel beside me at the altar and God would bless us both. It was such a long time ago that I had forgotten all about it.

The enemy of my soul knew that I was waiting on the Lord, and at the appointed time the vision would be fulfilled. Watch out, the devil hates those who wait patiently to receive from the Lord. The longer you wait patiently, the more your character and faith is built up in the Lord, as it was with our father Abraham. When one is tested by God, one's reaction after passing the test is a heart filled with joy and gratitude, ever praising and giving thanks to God. Remember, God makes everything beautiful in His time.

Chapter 18

Remembering An Impartation

Something that helped me during my time in London, waiting for the right husband and serving the Lord, was remembering all that I had learnt while back in Nigeria. I now had the chance to put that training into practice, as I learnt to trust the Lord through all the challenges of my new life.

In the year 2001, I had attended a leadership course in Shiloh. By that time, I had grown in faith in God's Word but still wanted more. Though I was living in Ghana at the time, I travelled to Nigeria to attend the course. I was the only female in a group of eight people. (I mentioned earlier how I was robbed of all my money on the way and testified how God miraculously provided for all my needs.) The speaker talked about the anointing and impartation received from God's faithful servants, who had shone their light victoriously in this dark world and had become successful in Christ. He shared a powerful testimony of how he sold his only car and used the money as a seed, which he sowed into the building and founding of his ministry. At one point, he was walking or using buses to travel to work and other places. But being at Shiloh in Nigeria, and seeing how vast the church building was, I saw a great reward for his humble beginnings and obedience to God's calling. I was touched and challenged by his testimony, so I decided to imitate his good works. I remember him giving some biblical examples of impartation. He spoke of handkerchiefs being distributed to the sick by Paul the apostle, and even in our days just touching the coats of anointed and godly men. As soon as he said that I imagined being the first to run up and touch his coat, if he called upon us to do so. I said a quiet prayer: "My Father in heaven, let me touch the bishop's coat for impartation, so that I would do exploits for thy Kingdom, just like him." As the bishop was still speaking to us, I fixed my eyes on his coat as I exercised faith that I would receive an impartation and return one day to share my testimony, to the glory of God. The sovereign God heard and answered my prayer.

After his teaching, he called the class to come and touch his coat because he had decided to anoint the class with oil on the last day of the course. I was the first to touch the bishop's coat. From that day, something happened to me. I had received an impartation from the man of God, and a seed of faith was sown into my life. I was marked from heaven for great things, though I did not know what the future had in store for me. It was just a matter of time before the seed that had been sown into my life would grow and bear fruit.

When I came to the UK, I put into practice what I had learnt by blessing everyone I came in contact with. From morning to night, my usual greeting went like this: "Bless you", or: "You are blessed and highly favoured." Remember, the Lord commanded us to bless and not to curse. One of the ways we are taught to experience God's blessings, as His children, is believing His promises and confessing them daily. I have been doing that for many years and I still continue to this day. I have experienced the power of God's Word in many ways as a result of my daily confession. (Proverbs 18:21, "Death and life are in the power of the tongue: and they that love it shall eat the fruit thereof.")

My way of greeting sounded strange to people, and it seemed like I was the only one greeting people everywhere. Although people were reluctant to respond, some would turn back and say thank you. Some asked, "Oh! Am I blessed?" In reply, I would say, "Yes and the Lord Jesus loves you", and with a smile they went away. Nothing stopped me from continually sowing seeds of blessing into people's lives.

It is said that whatever a person sows they will reap. Within three years, people started calling me "Highly Blessed." This reminded me of back home in Ghana, where we were taught to greet people at any time, and in response you received the same greeting. I began to think how amazing it was for people to call me "Highly Blessed." This was not something I claimed about myself. It brought to my mind the prophecy I received many years ago, when I was in Nigeria, that I would be addressed by good names. If you treat others well, with love, by your words and actions, you will receive the same response. I began to feel I was highly blessed, despite the fact that I was still going through five years of immigration problems, a situation my family and I had not foreseen. We had thought it would only take six months, or at most a year, for my immigration issue to be resolved.

I was not moved by the circumstances, but thought it was a good time for me to spread the Gospel and give out tracts to people around London. I just loved doing the Kingdom of God's business, because there was no pressure from anybody, and also because I had been anointed and called to evangelise. The anointing breaks the yoke. (Isaiah 10:27)

Chapter 19

God Works Behind The Scenes

During that period of evangelising in London, at one point I walked past a bridal shop. It attracted my attention. I entered and found a beautiful gown that I desired to wear on my wedding day. I spoke to the shop owner, who was very nice and a believer in Christ. I told her of my desire to marry one day, though I was yet to meet the man. Due to her good sales talk and words of encouragement, I decided to buy the gown. I negotiated the price of the gown, including all that I would need. I told her I was buying the gown in faith, believing that God would bring it to pass. The price was agreed, and I paid for it within six months. I also requested that the gown be kept for me, until the promise that God had given me was fulfilled. The shop owner said that she really admired my faith.

As I returned home with my receipt, I prayed to God saying: "I have bought this bridal gown by faith, and I present it before Thee, my Father, as faith and action to prove that I desire to marry. Holy Spirit, help me to pray about it until I receive an answer from the Lord. Remember Psalm 37:4-5, 'Delight thyself also in the LORD; and he shall give thee the desires of your heart. Commit thy way unto the LORD; trust also in him; and he shall bring it to pass." I wrote on a piece of paper the kind of man I wanted to marry and started confessing and praying about it.

I became tired of moving from one place to another, and finally desired to settle down. There was a "man with a van" who almost gave me a name, "Ms. Movement", but I rejected it in the name of our Lord Jesus! It will interest you to know that I moved fifteen times, to stay with different people in London. I did not pay for my accommodation, instead I helped by cleaning the place, wherever I lived. The only place I paid was in Bushey Hill Road, Camberwell. I believe it was the Lord's provision that I did not pay for accommodation in London for six years.

Those who know London well will understand how difficult it can be to find, let alone afford, rented accommodation, even a room in a shared house. People in steady employment can struggle to rent a decent home, and buying a property is now out of the reach of many. God made a way for me, despite my immigration status and lack of secure employment. Again and again, He provided a home for me just when I needed one. As an example of His provision, let me tell you how I came to be living in Bushey Hill Road.

For some time, my brother had been asking me to move out of his house, as his circumstances had changed and it was difficult for him to accommodate me. I had looked around, but not found anywhere suitable. This became very difficult for my brother, and eventually he had to ask me to leave. One evening, he told me to move out the following day or he would change the locks. I would no longer be allowed to enter his house. My brother also asked me to call on the Lord Jesus, who I served, and that He should give me a place. My brother said that he hadn't brought me into the world, and that my God should provide. I understood that what my brother said was true, and that I should trust God to provide, rather than rely on him. I am grateful for the time that I spent with my brother, but he was right that it was time for me to move on.

I took my brother's words seriously and went on my knees to cry out to God. Sometimes my brother jokes about things, but I realised that he meant what he said. I called my older brother in Ghana and explained my predicament. I said I would do all I could to find a place and asked to borrow a thousand pounds to help me secure a room. He kindly agreed to lend me the money, though arrangements would have to be made for it to be sent, so I wouldn't have it immediately. The next morning, I asked God to lead me, and I took a step of faith: I went into Peckham and wrote down the details of a number of rooms for rent, advertised in local shop windows. I then went home and prayed, before calling the phone numbers on the adverts. I asked God to guide me to the right place, which He had prepared for me. I was given the opportunity, after my phone calls, to view a number of rooms.

I went out again and viewed three rooms in shared houses, all in the local area. One of these rooms was too expensive for me, and the other rooms were too small. By the time I tried to view a fourth room, it was raining heavily and I couldn't get hold of the person who was renting the room to make arrangements. I had to go home again, soaked with rain. As soon as the rain stopped, I felt in my spirit that I should go back to the local shops, to check for further adverts. To my surprise, I found a number to ring that I did not recall seeing earlier. I phoned immediately and spoke to the landlord straight away. He explained that his house was nearby, in Peckham. He said I could walk there. He asked me to come about 4pm and said that he was expecting someone else to call who was also interested in the room. I went back home and cried out to God, as this house was very close to my brother and I didn't want to move far away. I prayed to God that He would give me favour, if this accommodation was His will for me.

At 4pm, I went back into the centre of Peckham and met the landlord at a nearby bus stop. He introduced himself as Yassa. We waited a few minutes for the other person viewing the room to arrive. As you can imagine, my heart was boiling! I was now desperate to be offered a room, before my brother changed the locks that evening. The three of us went to Yassa's house, on Bushey Hill Road. Yassa asked me to go and view the room first, as I had been the first to call him. When I went into the room, I found it was extremely large. There was a good bathroom and kitchen, just by the room, that we would share. I was happy with the house. After I had viewed the room, the other man also looked at it and wanted to rent it. But Yassa offered it to me, saying that I had contacted him first. So, God enabled me to find really good accommodation, in a central area of

London, in just one day! My Lord Jesus provided a place for me to live, as my brother said that He should.

In the evening, when my brother came home, he was amazed to find I had already found a place. Yassa had given me the keys, so I was able to show them to my brother. I moved in that weekend, and my brother helped me to move my things. I moved in without paying the rent, and Yassa didn't ask for a deposit. The money from my older brother in Ghana hadn't arrived yet. When my brother saw the room, he was amazed at how big it was, and that I had been given house keys before I had even paid the rent.

Yassa was a Moslem. He had separated from his wife and was going through a difficult time. I became a source of encouragement to him. I liked living with him, but I had to do a lot of cleaning, to keep the house in good order. I think he realised he needed some help with that, and that may be why he preferred a woman! Yassa was pleased that, after a while, I got his home sparkling clean. Yassa told me later that before I came to rent two men had taken the room and paid a deposit. However, he became suspicious that they might be drug dealers, so he gave them back their deposit and refused to let them move in. That was another reason he preferred a mature woman. When I had some work, I was able to buy and cook food, though sometimes Yassa would become hungry and eat it. However, he was fair to me, and deducted money from the rent due. I believe that it was God's will for me to live with Yassa, as it met an urgent need and turned out to be a wonderful location for me. It was near to my brother, and my nieces, and near to the Elim Pentecostal Church, where I finally met the husband that God had promised me.

Chapter 20

My MP's Visit To Elim Pentecostal Church

In December 2009, a friend informed me that my local MP, Ms Harriet Harman, was due to visit Elim Pentecostal Church, Camberwell. I had never heard of that church before but was very pleased to be given this information. My earnest desire was to see Ms Harriet personally, and also to express my sincere gratitude to her. My local MP and her team had written several letters to the Home Office on my behalf since May 2005.

After hearing this news about Ms Harriet, I prepared to attend the love feast. The occasion took place in a hired hall. I prayed that God would favour me, and I would be able to speak with her. I arrived at the venue very early and even helped to set up. Psalm 37:23 says: "The steps of a good man are ordered by the LORD: and He delighteth in his way." When we finished preparing the hall for the feast, as I turned around to go to the ladies, I met the senior pastor of the church. He greeted me and said that he had seen my face before. I reminded him that we had met at St. Giles Surgery, near Camberwell. I was sharing tracts on that day. As I gave him a tract, I had introduced myself as evangelist Claudia Joy, and he had told me that he was Pastor Sam Larbie of Elim Pentecostal.

I told him my reason for coming to the love feast. Since he was the right person, he assured me that if Ms. Harriet turned up he would make room for me to speak to her. I thanked him and told him I had prayed to God that she would come. He smiled and walked away. I spoke to God, thanking Him and singing praises. By then the love feast had already started. The praises went on and the atmosphere was filled with joy. The service was packed by the time Ms. Harriet and her team walked in. I was so happy to see my desire come true.

After the praise and worship, Pastor Larbie took the microphone and introduced the MP, who stood in front of the congregation. Pastor Larbie then told us the reason for her coming and, before he took his seat, he called me to the front and introduced me to Ms. Harriet. She received me with a warm hug, which amazed me. Praise the Lord! I had the opportunity to express my gratitude to her and her staff. She then asked me how far I had got with my immigration case. I told her that I had not received a reply since I submitted my appeal in 2007. She then assured me that she would see to the matter immediately. I thanked her once again and, as I was returning to my seat, Pastor Larbie gave me the microphone to testify to the church. "Help me Lord," I said to myself, "I did not plan this!" However, I took courage and testified how Ms. Harriet and her team had been helpful to me. I declared the blessing and salvation of our Lord Jesus Christ upon her life. As I walked back to my seat, I realised how wonderful and awesome my God had been, to enable me to meet Ms. Harriet.

(I know now that my future husband was there on that day! He also helped to set up the hall, and he remembers me coming forward to meet Ms. Harriet. However, we did not sit on the same table or speak to each other. That was the first time he ever saw me.)

Chapter 21
Time To Sign On At Becket House

As a result of my meeting with Ms Harriet, I received a reply from the Home Office within a week. It was so promising that I thought my indefinite leave to remain was in the post. While I was waiting for it, I got a letter from the Citizens Advice Bureau, where I had received some help from a solicitor who was no longer working with the Bureau. The letter instructed me to report at Becket House, an Immigration Office in London. That is a place where people without residence permits go and sign on daily, or weekly, depending on the individual's case. Offenders against immigration law could also be detained there by the authorities and sent back to their country of origin. I reported at Becket House. I was told to sign on every Monday, and that I was not allowed to work in the UK. I was also advised to employ the service of a solicitor to continue with my case. Because I did not have a current solicitor, I was in danger of being sent back home to Ghana. Fortunately, I was able to employ the services of a lady solicitor in my church. She sent my application afresh to the Home Office, including a photocopy of the recent reply I had received.

I started signing on at Becket House in February 2010. That was the start of a new trial, although I had received the word of promise from God. For three months I was signing on every Monday. At the beginning, I thought it would soon be over. After six months, without any news from the Home Office, I started fasting and prayer. I asked the Lord to do something about the situation. My solicitor had also told me not to break the immigration laws or I would face the consequences. At Becket House it felt like people were being punished for no reason. There were always more than a hundred people in a long queue outside. There was no shelter for anyone, even in winter or when it rained.

One day, while I was in the queue waiting to sign on, there was a heavy downpour which soaked my whole body. Within three days my right toe was swollen as a result of the rain, but I had to go and report at Becket House as usual. That particular day, I was blessed and highly favoured. The officer I spoke to was extremely kind to me. I showed him my swollen foot, and he wrote a note for me to go and see my GP and bring back the report. My GP directed me to go for an X-ray. The result showed that my right little toe had become infected because of my badly soaked boot in the rain. This was the exact report from my GP: "This lady has been registered at this practice since 2004 and is known to be of good character. She suffers from pain in the right great toe, due to osteoarthritis, and has recurrent Tinea Pedis in her feet."

When I sent the report, I was given permission to sign on every two months. What an answer to prayer! I saw the gracious hand of God in this. You may recall the story about my right little toe that got scalded, and how my dad stopped talking to my mum. It was not until I could walk properly that my dad started speaking to her. Today, both of them are no more but the report from my GP paved the way for me to enjoy some freedom. There is always a reason and a purpose for what happens to us in life. I have learnt not to be anxious about anything and also not to blame anyone for whatever happens. No one knows tomorrow. It is only God who knows our future and though it was painful for me to burn my foot as a baby, God knew it would favour me someday. It brought me a great liberty when I was released from signing on weekly and only had to report every two months. I continued signing on for three and half years.

90

Chapter 22

Time To Meet My Future Husband

Elim Pentecostal Church was close to Bushey Hill Road, Peckham, where I then lived. Indeed, I lived within walking distance of the Church. I was pleased with the kind attitude of the senior pastor, when I met him at the love feast. I decided to visit the church in January 2010. On my first visit, I was given a very warm welcome and that encouraged me to start attending their evening service. During one of their evening services, I shared my testimony of how I chose to live a righteous life in the sight of God and trust Him for His provision, rather than to lie and to have a job. (While I was still signing on at Becket House, I was not given any benefits and I was not allowed to work. But how could I survive in this country without work? Unfortunately, the elderly couple I was caring for had gone back to Ghana.)

After the service, the man to be my husband came and gave me £20. He said that was all the money he had in his pocket. "You may need it to buy something," he said. I was overwhelmed, because I did not expect money from anybody. He was the only white person among over three hundred people in the congregation. I have a confession to make. When I started attending the Elim Church, and I realised that he was the only white person, I commented to myself saying, "What is this man doing here? Could he not find a church with more white people to attend?" Well, the answer is my story, the crown of my testimony I am sharing with you now. The Lord God ordered my steps to where my husband could find me, for with God all things are possible.

Chapter 23

Time To Sow And Reap

I went through the membership class and became a full member of the Elim Pentecostal Church. I was encouraged to exercise my spiritual gift, by prophesying during the church services. I did not take this lightly. I acknowledged that one day all believers would give an account for their use of the gifts given to them by the Lord Jesus. As believers we are commissioned to preach the Gospel to the world, and I was so glad that the church went out to evangelise in the community. The leader of the evangelism team sometimes paired my future husband and myself together. It was a period of hard times for me because I was not working. I did my best to walk in faith. I was believing God for my indefinite stay in the UK, to enable me travel to Ghana. Many of the Elim members said to me, "If you did not tell us about your predicament, we would never know, because you are always so joyful." I lived in a way that was true to my new name, Joy, and delighted myself in the Lord. I kept praising and dancing to the Lord in all the church services.

I had only twenty-one pounds on a particular Sunday, and I had to buy my bus pass and use the remaining money for my shopping. I did not know where my next money would come from. During the offering time, I put one pound in the envelope and sealed it, but before I put it in the offering bowl the Holy Spirit said to me, "Why did you put the pound and not the twenty pounds? Are you not the one who prophesied: 'Give, and it shall be given unto you; good measure, pressed down, and shaken together, and running over, shall men give into your bosom. For with the measure that ye mete withal it shall be measured to you again.'" (Luke 6:38) As soon as I felt the prompting of the Holy Spirit, I removed the pound and put in the twenty pounds. I stayed after the service and enjoyed food and fellowship because there was a meeting in the evening. It was a monthly service known as the praise party. I never missed it, and always gave the Lord a good dance. I put the remaining pound in the offering and trusted God to provide for me, as I believed that the Holy Spirit had spoken to me.

After the service, a lady evangelist came and asked me if my name was Aba. I replied: "Yes". (Because I was born on a Thursday, my traditional Ghanaian name is Aba. Every woman in my tribe, Fante, who is born on that day of the week, shares that name.) She said that the Holy Spirit had told her to pray for me to receive a miracle. I quickly agreed with her, and she prayed with me. It was a surprise and made me realise how close the Lord was to me, caring for me in my situation. After the prayer, the next person I saw was Pastor Larbie, who started smiling at me. I returned the smile, as you can imagine, and he handed me an envelope, followed by his usual joke, "Get out of here!"

When I went outside the church, I checked how much money was in the envelope. It was twenty pounds! I felt really good because I had obeyed the Holy Spirit. I was full of joy that day. Sowing and reaping! I began to see that God was revealing Himself to me, so that I would continue to put my trust in Him alone. Nobody knew that I had put all the money I had into the offering. At the end of the day, I went home blessed with twenty pounds, rejoicing and praising God. It was a real miracle that I will never forget. Do not forget the Bible says: "The just shall live by faith." (Romans 1:17) From that day on, I moved to another level of faith in God. I also realised that trust and obedience is the key. It does not matter if it is only a small command. God can do anything, even beyond our imagination. Keep sowing and reaping! "Cast thy bread upon the waters: for thou shalt find it after many days." (Ecclesiastes 11:1)

In March 2012, during our Easter service, the word of the Lord came that we should all bring a thanksgiving offering. Everybody was asked to give as much as they were able to. I took this word very seriously. I counted my blessings, and I considered how far the Lord had brought me. If it had not been for the Lord's grace and His purpose for my life, I would have been sent back to Ghana. I thought that the Lord deserved a worthy thanks offering from me. I was fifty–four years old by then and had forgotten about my wedding gown with the shop owner. I rarely mentioned marriage in my prayers as after praying for three years the right man had not turned up. The enemy reminded me how old I was, and also pointed out to me how many young ladies were unmarried in our church. I was just believing God for my stay in the UK. All the money I had left was for my immigration payment, should I ever hear from them. Yet as I considered the word from God, I realised that God knew all my needs and was bigger than all my problems. If He said that we should bring a thanksgiving offering, why should I withhold anything from Him? Without a second thought, I put all my savings in an envelope, prayed over it, and took it to the church as my offering.

For the next two Sundays, I followed up my offering with dance, praise and worship to the Lord. Because I wore my Ghanaian kente cloth on those days, some members of the congregation asked me if it was my birthday, or a special occasion. I told them I was giving glory to God for His goodness towards me. I had learnt that God deserves all our praises, both before and after our breakthroughs. We must not forget that God will also test the intents of our hearts, as He did with Joseph. "Until the time of his word came: the word of the LORD tried him." (Psalm 105:19)

On the 29th March 2012, a member of our church, Brother Joe Lamptey, gave me a word from the Lord. I met him during his lunch break at McDonald's. He was a brother who encouraged me to continue exercising my spiritual gift by prophesying, and not to be afraid. We had a chat, encouraging each other in Christ. After that, he told me that the Lord said He was going to do something for me in April and crown it in September. He said, "Make sure you write it down, so that you do not forget, and pray about it." I am giving you this information for you to know that the God I am writing about is real. He performs wonders, and before they come to pass He tells you about them. Brother Joe gave me this message without knowing anything about my heart's desire, but God can use anybody to speak to you about your future, at His own appointed time. I received the prophecy by faith and wondered what exactly God was going to do for me. I wrote it down and began to pray about it. I continued to delight myself in the Lord. God is looking for people who delight themselves in Him, so that He will give them the desires of their heart. The fact that God sent somebody to me, made me feel blessed and highly favoured.

By that time, I was no longer living in Bushey Hill Road with Yassa. A member of the Elim Church, Aunty Margaret, invited me to come and stay at her house, as she was going away on a cruise and wanted to ensure that it was safe and secure. She gave me some money in advance, to thank me for looking after her home. This blessing assured me that my thanksgiving offering had been accepted by my Father God. Aunty Margaret didn't know that I had put all my savings into a thanksgiving offering, and she could have given me this money on her return, leaving me without money to live on. After she came back, I continued to live with her. She was happy to have help cleaning her home and cooking and invited me to stay. I didn't have to pay rent, so it was much easier for me.

I had a dream while Aunty Margaret was away. In the dream, I saw only the legs of a man sitting, wearing light khaki trousers, who called me to come and sit on his lap. I said, in the dream, "Who is this man asking me to come and sit on his lap? Eh! Then this man will really love me very well." I thought about this dream, because I remembered it so clearly, but nothing occurred to me about marriage. My mind was far away from marriage at the time. I had no residence permit in this country, and I was not working. Also, my understanding was that I would have to return to Ghana to marry, because of my circumstances in the UK.

Chapter 24
My Future Husband Spoke To My Pastor

I had now been in the Elim Church for three and a half years. I enjoyed being there, especially during the praise party service at the beginning of each month. On the 22nd April 2012, I received a text message from Brother Matthew, the only white man in the church, after he had spoken to our senior pastor. According to the text, he wanted us to start a relationship. When I read the text I did not understand it, so I called my pastor and asked him what it was about. His reply was, "Claudia Joy, the text you received is true. I am aware of it. Matthew came and spoke to me after the service. What I can tell you about him is that he is prayerful and a good Christian. He loves the Lord Jesus. And I know you are also single and waiting on the Lord for a good husband. Pray about it and let your heart decide. If you are interested, let him know." As he spoke, I felt calm and at peace. I thanked the pastor when we finished talking. I knelt down in prayer and said, "Father, thank you and have your way in this matter." I read the text again line by line and pondered over it. I was alone in Aunty Margaret's house because she was still on the cruise. That night I prayed, danced, and worshipped the Lord with great joy before going to bed.

Early in the morning, when I woke up, I read my Bible as I always do, to hear what the Lord had for me that day. I have been doing this for the past twenty years, and every page of my Bible is marked. As soon as I open my Bible I know exactly what the Lord is saying to me, as I am always full of expectation. That day, I opened my Bible and read Proverbs 18:22. "Whoso findeth a wife findeth a good thing, and obtaineth favour of the LORD." I immediately knew my Lord had spoken. That is why it is good to stay close to God and keep a right heart, so that we can hear Him when He speaks. Whenever we sin, we should quickly repent, as children of God, and continue in right relationship with Him.

He is the God that answers prayer. Later in the day, my pastor called me and asked me if I had an answer for Matthew, because he said it was not good to leave him without a reply. My heart was at peace, as I believed the Lord had spoken to me, and I felt I should not keep Matthew in suspense. I also remembered the prophecy given about something happening in April, and I considered how quickly that had come to pass.

Later, in the night, I sent Matthew a reply that since our pastor was aware of the text, and I had also received a word from the Lord that morning, we should give it a try. As soon as I sent the text, he replied by thanking me, with an invitation for dinner during the week. But when I told my pastor, he said we were not allowed to meet until our families had given their consent and the relationship was announced to the church. I was very pleased about that, because I did not want any embarrassment if the consent was not given. I was conscious of my immigration status, that I was not working, and that Matthew was white.

We were both invited to the church, on the Wednesday after I received the text, and met with the pastor to discuss things further. On that Wednesday, I asked the Lord for a sign. I said: "Father, if this is the right man, if he is the answer to my prayer, then please let him bring me some money for the week." I had no savings and had to live by faith, trusting the Lord at all times. I was completely amazed when Matthew gave me twenty pounds, as soon as we met in the church. This was the second time he gave me money without me asking him. I was overwhelmed! I said nothing to him about my prayer but thanked him. We met the pastor in his office. He explained how relationships at the Church were important and not taken lightly. Matthew told me he had to fast and pray for a day before he called his dad about the relationship. His dad is also a born-again believer in Christ. His father's reply was that it was an answer to his prayers. He sent his letter of approval by email.

Both my parents have gone to be with the Lord. The senior member of our family is my cousin, who is a dentist in London. He was on holiday, so I waited till he came back. Every member of my family was glad to hear about my exciting news, and my cousin happily wrote his letter of approval when he returned. Matthew said his siblings were shocked when he told them, because he had said he wasn't going to get married. They were delighted and have always given us their full support.

After the responses from our families were received, a date was fixed for our introduction to the congregation. On the day of our announcement, 6th May 2012, the whole church was filled with great joy. We stayed for both the morning services, and so our new relationship was announced twice. Those who were there for both services, and knew what the announcement in the second service was going to be, pretended that they didn't know, to keep it as a surprise. Pastor Larbie called Matthew up to the front first, and the congregation erupted into loud cheers, applause and shouting, as he came up. He was the last person they were expecting to come to the front for a new relationship to be made public: the only white man in the church, in his fifties, and known to be a confirmed bachelor.

The church had never had an inter-racial relationship before. People were delighted and expressed their delight very loudly! The drums were hit, cymbals clanged, and all the instruments played, including the saxophone that was such a feature of worship at Elim Camberwell. Pastor Larbie milked the moment and delayed asking me to come to the front, to keep the excitement going. He even said that he had changed his mind and would announce the lady the following week. Several members of the church then rushed to the front and pleaded with him to let them know who the lady was. Finally, he asked me to come and join Matthew, and I came forward to even more exuberant praise, shouting and applause. I remember hearing a whistle that the pastor's wife was blowing. After we were prayed for, many people came forward to hug us, and to congratulate us. I remember Brother Friday, a very large man who was much loved in the church, lifting me up so that my feet left the floor, as a father might lift his young daughter. Brother Friday later helped us to organise our wedding, as we made him our "Chairman". Having a Chairman is common practice in Nigeria and Ghana, and this person fills an important role, helping to keep arrangements on track, but also providing financial assistance if needed. The Chairman does not supplant the best man and the maid of honour, but works alongside them, on behalf of both of the families. The announcement of our relationship was an occasion that we will always remember. It was the doing of the Lord, and it was marvellous in our eyes. We were told not to meet each other at home. We were to meet in places like McDonald's, KFC, Burger King, and public parks. In this way, we would avoid any temptations, before we were joined together as a couple.

After the service, two young girls came to us, and said they would love to be our flower girls on our wedding day. Sister Yemisi also promised to make our wedding cake as a gift. How grateful we were to receive a video clip of our announcement, from the brother who later filmed our wedding. We started courting from that day. We began to fall in love day after day, as we met to talk, and got to know each other better. One thing I knew for sure about our relationship was that God's hand was on it, because my husband did not worry about my immigration status. The more we talked about my situation, the more he encouraged me that the Lord would make a way for us. I found him to be a kind and generous person. As a natural giver myself, I was blessed to meet a man who was also a generous giver. He took full responsibility for my daily needs, because I was not working, during our courtship.

Only a few weeks after we started courting, we had an incident of racial abuse. We were standing chatting on the street, before parting company to go home. There happened to be a pub nearby, although we hadn't been in it. The pub was in Denmark Hill, South London. A man came out of the pub and said to us, "These mixed relationships just don't work. I'm sorry, but they just don't work." He sounded angry and aggressive and had clearly been drinking. We were stunned into silence. As this happened so early in our relationship, we were concerned this indicated the shape of things to come! That concern was heightened shortly afterwards, when Matthew was hit by an egg, thrown at him as he sat in an internet café in Camberwell, near to the Elim church. This happened before a prayer meeting that we were both attending, which he had to attend with egg stains on his clothes. All the church members at the meeting were concerned. It was worrying that this happened in Camberwell, where we were spending much time in restaurants and cafes together. The incident was reported to the police, and it was investigated. However, it transpired that the person who threw the egg had a grudge against the internet café and was a known troublemaker. There was no evidence that he was targeting Matthew. And the racist incident turned out to be a one-off. We found that people were interested when they saw us together, and often made remarks, but those were rarely hostile. During the time we have been together, inter-racial relationships have become more and more common in London.

Chapter 25

Time To Tell My Future Husband

After I thought about all that had happened, I concluded that Matthew was a man of action with a good heart. I had no doubt about him, as he had won my heart. For this reason, I did not hesitate to tell him about money I had back home in Ghana. This money was in a long-term bond, set up by my brother, and I had not been able to access it until now. My family thought it would provide for me, if I had to return home again. It was my share of the money from the sale of land the family had owned. This land had turned out to be valuable, as it was in a central area of Accra, near to the airport. I wasn't involved in the decisions about that but was grateful that this long-term bond had matured, and I could finally use it to meet our current needs. Matthew could not believe it when I told him. I was the last person whom he thought would possess such a large sum of money. A blessing which the Lord had prepared for us. He then told me how the Lord had promised him, as an answer to his prayers, that he would own a home in the immediate future. He had no idea how he could afford it, looking at his salary and house prices in London. It may interest you to know that Matthew had also moved about ten times as a bachelor, to rent in different places, just like me. Before we got married, the Lord brought our finances together, and gave us our own miracle home.

Let me tell you the story of how my husband received the promise of God, that he would have his own home very soon. My husband works in social care, with people with learning disabilities, a worthwhile field of work, but not well paid compared to many professions. He did not have any savings, or any deposit to buy a home. The accommodation he was living in was unsatisfactory, but having moved so many times, he was reluctant to move to another rented place yet again. He sought the Lord in prayer and was sure that the Lord had heard his prayer and granted his request. He prayed that God would give him his own flat, with the furniture already in it. As he was so sure that he had heard from God, he didn't want to repeat his request, as if it had not been granted, and doubt God. But the situation he was in was difficult, and he needed to move urgently. So, he set aside a day to fast and pray, and ask God to move quickly. He knew he had a promise from God, but not how long it would take for it to be fulfilled. Later that day, he listened to a sermon by one of his favourite preachers, T. D. Jakes, which he had never heard before. It was called "Immediately". It spoke to him powerfully, and he knew that God was saying he would not have to wait too long until he had his own flat. Within eighteen months of hearing that message, he had met me, and we had married and bought our home together: our own flat, with the furniture already in it.

Chapter 26

My Faith Wedding Gown And Engagement

Weeks after Matthew and I were introduced to the church, I went to Mrs Sola Ekerin, the owner of a bridal shop that is still operating inside East Street Market, London. It was over four years since my last visit. She did not recognise me when I first entered and greeted her. Her reaction went like this: "Eh....eh... eh", as she opened her mouth. "Excuse me, Sister, are you still in this country? It is almost five years since 2008. We are in 2012. Are you the same sister who bought the gown, or are you her ghost?" She took a good look at me, as I showed her my receipt, and finally said, "You are welcome, and now, tell me what happened to you." Before I opened my mouth to speak, she interrupted saying, "I thought you had gone back to Ghana." I told her my story briefly. She then embraced me with joy and a song of victory! This was the song: "This kind God oh, I never see your kind oh, this kind God oh, blessed be your Holy Name." It was followed by, "He is a miracle working God, He is the miracle working God, He is the Alpha and Omega, He is the miracle working God." I told her that for four years, God was working a miracle in His own time, for me to come to this point. That is why we need to be patient in all things. God gives you the best when you wait on Him. She was so excited! "God deyoooooooo!" She shouted again and again.

She then told me how she had sold my gown, after three years, when she did not see or hear from me. She said it was the doing of the Lord, because anything could have happened, and I might not have come back to the shop. I agreed with her. With a big smile on her face, she promised that on her next trip to the US she would order a new wedding gown. I was so grateful to hear that, and we both gave thanks and glory to God. She said if it was someone else she would not bother about it, because it was not her fault. Yet after the miracle that she had heard from me, she wanted to buy a more beautiful gown than the one she had sold. She assured me I was not going to pay any money, even if the new one should cost her more. She was such a blessing!

Matthew and I got closer, as we introduced our families to each other. My future daddy-in-law came to visit our church, some weeks after we were announced. The congregation were excited when he came. He met the senior pastor after the service and we took some pictures with him. I believe he enjoyed himself, as Matthew and I took him to lunch after that unique service. The introduction to our families went further when we visited my cousin in Woking. We also visited my future husband's senior brother Rod, and partner sister Jess, in London Bridge. We then went to my older brother Dr S. K. Arthur and his lovely wife. We encountered some challenges, but we also had wonderful times talking and praying together. I remember the day we sat in McDonald's for nine hours, and it seemed like just an hour. We were the talk of the town, as people made comments about us when we walked together to church and other places. 'Newlyweds' was the term used for us, even though we were courting at that time. We also visited the park often because Matthew loves to spend time there.

Matthew and I were engaged on Saturday the 8th September 2012. The timing of our engagement fulfilled the word of prophecy. By then, we had been in a relationship for six months. My future daddy-in-law and Matthew went on the internet and learnt about engagement rites in Ghana. Our families were informed, and plans were made for a low-key ceremony. On our engagement day, everything went smoothly for us, by God's grace. The engagement took place at 197, Cator Street, in Peckham, where I had lived with my brother Atta and my two nieces. It was a beautiful sunny day. My family and some leaders from the church were already waiting when, at 1 .00 pm, we heard "Agooo! Knocking at the door!" It was Matthew, his family, Brother Philip and his wife Sister Herty. They had come to take their "special flower", the bride. Brother Philip and Sister Herty had come from the church to help Matthew on the day. They arrived with my dowry, engagement gifts, ring, Bible, suitcases, cloths, and assorted drinks.

Without wasting any time, the MC started the ceremony, after prayers were said. Because the ceremony was performed in the living room, only a small number of people were invited for the occasion. I was called in and revealed to Matthew who, after we had been prayed for, put the engagement ring on my finger. It was the happiest day of my life. Words were not enough for me to express my joy. I was so blessed to see a few of my old secondary school friends, who came with a surprise cake for us. (These old school friends also now live in the UK.) Some other friends of mine, who heard about our engagement, came without invitation. They called themselves "Genuine Gate Crashers." They told me later, that they could not afford to miss the occasion they have been praying about for so long. It was the joke of the day. Food and drinks were served and both families chatted together, and pictures were taken. The next day, the whole church was informed. My engagement ring was shown round as evidence of the ceremony. To God be all the glory!

Chapter 27
Finding Our Miracle Home

After our engagement, we agreed to take out a mortgage and buy a home by faith. We had been praying about it since I told my husband about my bond in Ghana. We both desired to be in our own home. We started looking for a place to buy. During our search, our church purchased a bigger building near Catford. We therefore targeted areas around Bromley and Grove Park. Our mortgage broker suggested Santander could be the best bank for us, as they were more favourable to older first-time buyers. My situation, the age of my husband, and having to take a mortgage on his salary alone, was enough to put us in fear of being denied a mortgage. We knew it would take a miracle for us to buy a home. Nevertheless, we both believed God. I wrote down the type of home we wanted: a two-bedroom ground floor flat with a garden. My husband spent most of his time in an internet café, searching for homes we could go and view. We viewed some places across South London, but none of them were for us.

Before a promise from God is fulfilled, and we receive the promised Isaac, there is often an Ishmael that comes along, to lead us astray. At one point, we did find a flat that we both loved. It was in Hither Green, South East London, ground floor, and had large rooms and a long garden with two sheds. We were on a tight budget. But the guide price was very reasonable, as it was a "repossession". (The previous owners had been unable to keep up with the mortgage payments, and the mortgage provider was now selling the property.) Because of that, the time allowed to complete the purchase was greatly reduced. We were excited, and quickly made an offer. The estate agent encouraged us to come in at a low price, as he felt that would be accepted to ensure a quick sale. However, we soon found that we were competing against a cash buyer, who outbid us, with a very attractive offer.

At the time we were disappointed, but in fact this turned out to be a deliverance. We were trying to move my money from a bank in Ghana, which turned out to be difficult. Although it was now possible to access that money, as the bond had finally matured, the bank was reluctant to release it. They kept asking for more details, including an invoice to prove we had bought a flat! Pastor Alfred, the administrator and assistant pastor at Elim Camberwell, helped us at that time, contacting a manager at the bank, who he had known some time ago when he still lived in Ghana. I also managed to get a letter from the mortgage broker that we were using, confirming that we were buying a property in London. However, when I later spoke to his boss, he was unhappy the mortgage broker had written the letter, as he didn't want him to get involved. That made it difficult for the mortgage broker to continue to represent us.

Matthew then found a flat on the Bromley Road, and we went for a viewing on the 22nd December. At 11.00am, we knocked on the door of the flat. The seller received us with some excitement. As soon as we saw the rooms and the garden, we knew that it was for us. God gave us favour with the negotiation, and within five minutes the deal was done. He had time to show us round, and he even gave me the keys to the garden. We agreed on the price, including the contents of the flat, which was amazing. The sale included a television, living room furniture, fridge freezer, gas cooker, washing machine, hoover, iron, wardrobes, curtains, kitchen utensils, plates and glasses, and garden equipment. The seller told us how he had asked his niece to come and take the washing machine for free, but she did not turn up. We knew it was the good pleasure of our Father in heaven to bless us with it. We were the right people to purchase the flat with the contents, including the washing machine. The seller told us that it was his old mum who had lived in the flat. He told us how clean and tidy his mum had been. I replied that she sounded just like me. Before we left, he told us we were the first to come and view and he was pleased to sell to us. He said he had accepted our offer and was prepared to remove the property from the market. The price we agreed was very reasonable, and the value of the flat has increased greatly since we bought it.

After we had found the property, we still hadn't found a mortgage. We did not give up, and Matthew kept making calls to different branches of Santander. This happened around Christmas time, and it was difficult to arrange an appointment as so many staff were on leave and the banks were closed on the bank holidays. Matthew was staying with his dad in Dorset, and he made the calls from there, updating me all the time, as I prayed to God to help us. He finally got an appointment with a mortgage adviser at the Peckham branch. Matthew asked me to accompany him, because the adviser happened to be a Ghanaian. I was reluctant to go, because I thought the bank would question me about my stay. However, on second thoughts, I realised that God could favour me, and so I went. When I met the lady adviser, it turned out that our grandparents were from the same town in Ghana. She treated me like a long lost relative, as we talked about Ghana. Matthew even said she looked a bit like me, with the same exuberant personality! The God of favour favoured us in her sight and she did everything she could to get us a mortgage, despite all the odds. We spent five and a half hours at the bank. We arrived at 2.00pm and left at 7.30pm, when the bank had already closed. We were so happy and grateful to God, as well as to the mortgage adviser.

Chapter 28

I Remembered The Promise God Gave Me

The time had come for the promises of God to be fulfilled. I remembered the prophecy given to me 27 years ago, about a noble man kneeling beside me at the altar and God blessing us together. The experience of waiting for the fulfilment of a promise must come to an end. As the saying goes: "no condition is permanent." Psalm 30:5 reads, "Weeping may endure for a night, but joy cometh in the morning." I felt as if scales on my eyes had been removed. Once I was blind but now I could see. I felt the words in Psalm 102:13 spoke directly to me. ("Thou shalt arise, and have mercy upon Zion: (Claudia Joy) for the time to favour her, yea the set time is come.") I said to the Lord, it is now my turn, favour me now! Indeed, all my daily needs were met, as if I had never gone through the experience of lack. I was blessed and highly favoured wherever I set my feet. I did not stop confessing the truth of the prophecy.

Matthew and I believed in prayer. With thanksgiving, we carried all our supplications to the Lord. As Christians, we have a part to play by communicating with God. God does not need our help. We need His help. It is our duty therefore to pray without ceasing. (1st Thessalonians 5:17) After a successful engagement ceremony, we started trusting God for our wedding. We had not heard any news from the Home Office for over a year. We wrote and informed them about our change of circumstance through my MP. I continued to sign on at Becket House. The enemy came like a flood into our situation, and played on my mind saying, "God Has performed what He said He would do for you in April and September, now we shall see how you will get married without your stay."

Without a permit from the marriage registrar, even our church could not marry us. But how could I get the permit when I was still signing on at Becket House? Matthew and I believed God, and we decided to put our faith into action. We called the marriage registry office, and we were given an appointment. We had prayed and trusted God would help us. On that day, we took all the necessary documents I had with us. We got there in good time and waited to be called. After a short wait, a lady came and called us to her office. She looked through my papers and said there was only one paper missing, which was an IPS96. She told us if I could get that form, she would start the process to enable us to obtain our permit to marry. When I heard that, I gave a sigh of relief, because I feared my husband could only marry me in Ghana. I asked her to explain what the form was and how to get it. She said it was a document giving proof of identity, with my photograph, that I could get from Becket House. I said to Matthew, I must get this form today and submit it to her. It was not my day to sign on, but I asked Matthew to accompany me, though he was a bit reluctant to go. We prayed for favour and went to Becket House.

When we arrived at Becket House, I showed the officer my signing on form. He said, "What do you want here? Today is not your day to sign on." I explained why we had come. He looked at my face and asked Matthew to stand outside, and he directed me to join the queue inside. I thought that was promising, and my face beamed with a smile. When it was my turn to speak to the officer at the counter, he also asked why I was there. I told him what brought me. He directed me to go and have my photograph taken. He then signed the new IPS96 form with my photo on it. It took less than five minutes, and I was out of the place. Matthew could not believe I had been given the right form. I told him we would only know if we took it to the lady at the registry office. When we returned to the registry office, they were on break. So, we went to a nearby restaurant to have some snacks.

While we were waiting, after our food, I checked my phone to see if I had received a call. I had received a voicemail from the solicitor from my former church. She said the Home Office had written to her, and she had sent their letter on to me. When I told Matthew, we looked at each other, and could not believe what was going on! The registry office had resumed after the lunch break, so we went and gave the IPS96 form to the lady. As soon as she saw it, she said "Yes! That is what I was looking for." Praise the Living God! She was pleased we were able to get it, as she said that many others in our situation do not. She gave us the marriage permit form to fill in, and after that we paid for it to be processed. We returned home that day thanking and praising the Lord our God.

The next day, I received the letter from the Home Office. I was overjoyed to read that letter. It contained a form to fill in and return with four passport size photos. If you were in my shoes, what would you have expected next? My indefinite leave to remain of course! I did not receive it, but that Home Office letter came at the right time, and it gave us confidence to move on and prepare for our wedding. I still don't know how the Lord did it for us. He can do it for you too. Within twenty-one days, we got the permit for the church to marry us.

It was now clear that God was bringing His promise to fulfilment. We received the permit for marriage from the registry office with great joy and excitement. I took it to the leadership of our church, Elim Pentecostal, and they all rejoiced with us. Our wedding was arranged for the 16th March 2013. The Lord is so faithful. The congregation were shouting and jumping for joy when our wedding date was announced in the church. Many of the members pledged to help us, with soft drinks, small chops, bottled water, and help on the day. We wanted part of our wedding celebration to be like the monthly praise party, as we loved that so much. The praise and worship team were happy to help us with that. What can I say? Words cannot express it all.

A member called Brother Friday, who I mentioned earlier, invited me to an early morning prayer meeting. He was the speaker on that day. I went there, but he did not get the opportunity to speak. At the end, he told me the leader of the prayer meeting forgot to ask him. All the same, during the meeting, the only white lady in the church gave me a prophecy. She said, "Claudia Joy, the Lord says your wedding will be successful." It was a timely word from the Lord, and I received it with gratitude and expectation. I was glad Brother Friday had invited me. I told Matthew about the prophecy. With this word of assurance from the Lord, we were both certain that God was moving every stone to bring His word to pass, and no devil could stop it. I want to say here, "For since the beginning of the world men have not heard, nor perceived by the ear, neither hath the eye seen, O God, beside thee, what He hath prepared for him that waiteth for Him." (Isaiah 64:4)

I went to the owner of the bridal shop and informed her of the date of our wedding. She received the news with excitement, and she promised to get me the new gown before we married. Two weeks before our wedding, I received a call from the bridal shop owner. She invited me and Matthew to come and choose my gown. I prayed about it and asked the Lord to go before us and help me to make the right choice. When we got there, she had displayed about ten different gowns for me to choose from. I looked around carefully and pointed one out. Mrs Ekerin's eyes filled with tears. When I asked her why she was shedding tears, she replied that it was the new one she had bought with my measurements. But she wanted me to feel free to make my own choice. She was shedding tears of joy, on seeing the desires of my heart being fulfilled. She gave me an appointment to come and try it. We spoke privately, without my future husband hearing. We did not want him to see me wearing it until the big day. When I came and tried it, it was perfect. She also provided all the accessories needed.

You may wonder why I have written a lot about Mrs Ekerin and my wedding gown. But what I would have done on my wedding day without my gown? There was a Christian lady in the shop when I tried on my gown. She started prophesying Psalm 126:1,2,5 into my life. ("When the LORD turned again the captivity of Zion, (Claudia Joy), we were like them that dream. Then was our mouth filled with laughter, and our tongue filled with singing: then said they among the heathen, the LORD hath done great things for them. They that sow in tears shall reap in joy.") She was speaking as if she knew me from somewhere. She could not stop saying how I was blessed and highly favoured.

Chapter 29

Our Big Day On The 16th March 2013

The night before our wedding, my husband and I met, and we prayed together. We asked God to make our marriage and wedding day successful, for His glory. We trusted the Lord to fulfil His promise to us. We assured each other of our love. The next morning, I awoke with gratitude and joy filled my heart. My sister Dorothy, my nieces and my makeup artist were around to help me. We prayed together and committed the day into the hand of God. My video operator came on time and that alone lifted my spirit. The moment for joy and laughter had come. It was the day of smiles, "cheese" and click from the camera! The Lord had turned my mourning into dancing. The day was a demonstration of the verses in the book of Ecclesiastes 3:1;4. ("To everything there is a season, and a time to every purpose under the heaven: A time to weep, and a time to laugh; a time to mourn, and a time to dance.") God must always be sovereign over the events and seasons of our life. It is the Lord who decides when and how, for His glory.

The top priority, as we prepared to marry, was something I had desired all my adult life. My desire was to be driven in a Rolls Royce on my wedding day. Matthew was pleased when I mentioned it, and he made the arrangement as soon as possible. The funny thing was, on our wedding day, there was no time for us to be driven together in the Rolls Royce. He sat in a red double decker bus to get to the church. Oh! I did not like that, but I am sure he was so excited that he did not mind. He is such a good-hearted man who really cares for his wife. He enjoyed joking with his colleagues at work, on his return, that he had travelled to his wedding alone, on a 176 bus, while his wife came with her bridesmaids in a Rolls Royce. As it had been raining, and he was wearing a white suit, he had to be careful as he got off in Camberwell and walked to the church. His family all met him on arrival, having travelled from different places across the country. It was a great joy for them to see him on his wedding day, and something they had never expected.

Matthew and I were particular about the food to be served. We were so blessed to employ the service of a caterer, Aunty Adelaide, from our church. She was highly recommended, and we both agree that she did a good job. My sister, Mrs Dorothy Williams, was glad to decorate the church and to be my maid of honour. We asked two of my nieces, Mama and Nanaaba, to be my bridesmaids. They were the perfect choice to fulfil that role for me. They were very happy. As for Matthew, it was not easy for him to choose his best man. However, he decided that his elder brother Rod was much the best person to ask. By end of our wedding day, we were so grateful. He and his partner, Sister Jess, were a great blessing to us.

The venue of our wedding and reception was the Elim Pentecostal church, Camberwell. The time of the service was 1.00pm. I had been asked not to be late. I took that seriously and was ready to go to the church by 12.00 noon. The driver of my car came on time at 12.15pm. When I saw my Rolls Royce, I gave all my praises to God. Pictures were taken of me sitting inside the car, before I asked my sister and my nieces to join me. My two beautiful flower girls, Hannah Adedoyin and Omoye Moses, and page boy, Alexander Williams, my nephew, were waiting for us at the church. The church was full, and many were standing, with the choir ministering in songs when we arrived. There were little drops of rain, and I commented that they were showers of blessing, as I stepped out of the car. The driver politely brought an umbrella and covered me. I walked into the church on time. It was the day the Lord honoured me, and the congregation called out and shouted, "Blessed and highly favoured!"

Matthew came to meet me as I entered, bowed with honour and received me from the arm of my cousin, Dr Benjamin Annobil. He gave me away in the absence of my dad. The congregation were shouting with indescribable excitement. When the time came for "You may kiss the bride" all eyes were fixed on us. My husband, who by then was no longer nervous, stole the show and gave me the longest kiss on record. Pastor Alfred gave my husband a "high five". The congregation looked on and cheered with laughter and astonishment. There were over four hundred people at the wedding. My husband's family were so happy to see him marry me. My family were also pleased that I had married a born-again Christian from my own church. My brother, Dr S. K. Arthur, introduced a well-known song that he had written, Ebenezer. He dedicated it our mother, Madam Alexandra Arthur, saying that she would have loved to have been there. As my sister Dorothy led the congregation in song, my brother accompanied her on the keyboard. He is a gifted musician. A few of my friends shed tears of joy when we danced together as Mr and Mrs, as we went to sign our marriage certificate. We then returned to the praise party. The congregation danced with me on my special song: "Who has the final say? Jehovah has the final say. Who has the final say? Jehovah turned my life around, Jehovah turned my life around, He makes a way where there seems no way, Jehovah, has the final say!"

It was then time for us to go and take some pictures, but it was raining. I said aloud, "The devil is a liar! My God is good." I then told the video man that we would walk through the rain and take the pictures by faith. I said, just as the Lord stopped the sun in the days of Joshua, even so I believe He is able to stop the rain for us. I encouraged everybody, as I stepped into the rain, to come along. To the glory of God, when we all gathered, the rain stopped, and the sun shone brightly. We were able to take some memorable and beautiful pictures. We all clapped our hands, praising the Living God. Alleluia!

When we returned, we found a high table, beautifully prepared at the altar of the church. This fulfilled God's promise to bless us together at the altar. We dined and danced before our God, who deserves all the praise. Brother Joe Lamptey and Sister Kay Banful were the MCs for the day. Our cake was placed in front of the altar, by Sister Yemisi, who gave it to us. It was beautifully decorated, to match the colours we chose for the wedding. After the opening prayer, the floor was opened for speeches. I will always remember the lovely speech made by my niece, Ms Michelle Hagan (Nanaaba). My husband's best man, his elder brother Rod, was then called to give his speech. He made everyone laugh, and he ended by proposing the toast. My husband responded to the toast with a joke. He took the microphone, thanked everyone for coming, and sat down immediately. Everybody laughed! He then got up and gave his speech. His speech almost made me shed tears, as he thanked me for marrying him. He shocked everyone when he ended his speech, by singing a song in a Ghanaian dialect. ("Me dawa ase, ese se me dawa aseoo, ese se me dawa ase." We thank you oh Lord, we just want to thank you Lord, we just want to thank you Lord.)

We were then called to open the floor with a dance. I believe it was a good dance, as some people asked me if we had practiced it. Food was served, and everybody had enough to eat. Everyone in the church knew I loved dancing, so we were called to dance a second time. To our surprise, the Chairman of our reception showered on me a good amount of dollars. Don't forget, there is always a reward when you give the Lord a good dance. He causes men to bless you. My husband told me, after we married, that my dancing in church had encouraged him to speak to the pastor about me. So, we danced and danced until everyone joined in, especially the children. Finally, I gave my bouquet of flowers away by throwing it backwards, to be caught by the fortunate single to be married next. I don't know if that works. I think it is a joke!

The reception was brought to an end with a vote of thanks from Sister Kay Banful. We were blessed to see our wedding come to a successful end. Without my indefinite leave to remain, God turned my mourning into dancing. In fulfilment of the promise from God, I got married in the Lord at the age of fifty-four. We had booked a place in

Brunel Manor, a Christian Holiday and Conference Centre, for our honeymoon. There was a heavy downpour after our wedding, but we had made all the arrangements for our journey. We had a wonderful time at Brunel Manor. On the day we came back to London, we had a phone call from the solicitor, who told us that the purchase was completed, and the keys to our flat could be collected.

I want to explain why we had our reception in the church. It was our hearts desire to have a non-alcoholic reception. It also saved time, with no travel to another venue, and allowed us to have a longer time for praises and dancing, led by our own praise and worship team. The Good Lord satisfied our hearts desire, and brought the fulfilment of His promise, to bless us before His altar. God's Word cannot fail. If He said it, He will bring it to pass.

Chapter 30

Moving Into Our Miracle Home

We moved into our miracle home with joy and excitement. We invited one of our pastors and his wife to come and dedicate our home into the hands of God. The area God gave us is fantastic. Our GP is within walking distance, bus stops are close, and the train station is seven minutes away. There is a park opposite the railway station, and a regular Tuesday and Thursday market nearby. It took some time for us to settle in, as we had to change the carpets and purchase some new furniture.

The people in the area accepted us, and gradually we got to know our immediate neighbours. Through an unexpected incident, we met the man who lived above us: I was in the flat alone, when I heard water pouring down through our ceiling. I brought a bucket to collect it, and within seconds the bucket was full. I did not know what to say or what to do. I ran outside and met the lady who cleans the estate. When I told her, she replied "Don't be anxious about it. The Lord who brought you into the flat will take care of it." She realised that I was shaken. I had already talked to her about our testimony, and how the Lord had given us our miracle home. In the light of that, she spoke this word from the Lord that gave me peace. She then told me to go upstairs and tell the neighbour. When I told the man above us what had happened, he was shocked and apologised. His own kitchen was flooded, so I went back and brought some old towels and helped him to wipe his floor. We found out later that the flood was caused by the flat above his. When my husband returned home from work, and found the bucket filled with water, he could not believe it.

Then the enemy came with his lies, suggesting that if God had blessed us with our flat, it would not now be flooded with water. Friends, don't let the devil lie to you. There will always be unexpected problems in life. It is written in Psalm thirty-four, verse nineteen, "Many are the afflictions of the righteous: but the LORD delivereth him out of them all." We had been going through a lot, so we asked the Lord to intervene and help us. The Lord answered our prayer. We got to know more about our neighbour above, and we became close leaseholders. He gave a promise to pay for the damage caused to our ceiling, after we had made an insurance claim. The Lord gave us favour with the insurance company, and he did not have to pay us any money. Instead of repainting only the ceiling in our kitchen, we received enough money to enable us to redecorate the whole kitchen, bathroom and toilet as well. Our radiators were also repainted, and we only paid a small amount for that. The problem turned out to be a blessing. To God be all the glory.

Chapter 31

Immigration Problems Again:
A Powerful Testimony

We had been married for four months, when Prophets Ron and Jane Jollif visited London from Ohio, USA, in July 2013. I was excited because we had not seen them for over a year. We met and rejoiced over all the wonderful works that the Lord had done for my husband and I. Jane Jollif gave me a prophecy. She revealed that there was an immigration problem that I would go through, but the Lord would help me and I would not be sent back home. When she mentioned an immigration problem, I said to myself, "Even when I am now married to Matthew, and we are living in our own home?" "If the Lord had not been on our side, then the enemy would have swallowed us." (Psalm 124:1-3).

A week after the prophecy, I went to Becket House to sign on. The officer at the counter took my IPS96 identity form and asked me to follow him. I followed him to a place where he told me to remove my jacket and my handbag, for safe keeping. I was then given a big brown envelope to open and read the long-awaited decision on my case. To my amusement, my case was finally closed on 21st April 2013, a month after we were married. The shocking decision that had been made was that I should leave the UK and return to Ghana within 28 days, or I would be forced out. The case worker argued that my two nieces were now adults and they could always communicate with me in Ghana. I don't think I need to say any more for you to understand how I felt after I read that. But I remembered that the Lord had revealed a week ago that He would help me, and so I was calm and peaceful.

Fifteen minutes later, a lady came and called me to her office. She asked me to confirm that I was a Ghanaian. She then called the British embassy in Ghana for me to speak to someone. When I took the phone, my first question was, "What is going on?" The person answered and said I should speak in my Ghanaian dialect. So, I told him that I was married to a British man and we were living together. He told me I should ask my husband to act quickly, because if I did not leave the UK within 28 days I would be repatriated. The lady then took the phone from me. I tried to explain things to her, but she told me I should go and speak to my solicitor. How wonderful are the works of God. Our God reveals to redeem. I felt so much peace in my spirit on my way back home.

My husband had called me many times, but my phone was off. I got home and thanked God for His presence in my life. I committed the situation into His hand. I thanked God again for giving me a husband and home before the Home Office decision was taken in April. The fact that I did not receive this decision before the prophets came and foretold an immigration problem proves that my God is in control. He has the final say! I encourage you to put your trust in Him alone. I then placed the envelope on the kitchen table and jumped into the bath. A few minutes later, my husband came in and read through the decision while I was having my bath. By the time I finished, my husband was shouting "Praise the Lord! Alleluia!" He called me to come and have a look. He showed me where the decision said I had no family ties in the UK. This showed that the case worker was not informed of our engagement, or marriage.

My husband acted quickly. Initially, we got advice from a solicitor. She was not optimistic. She did advise that I should change my address with the Home Office, to make it clear we were living together. We then sent photocopies of all the letters that we had written through my local MP, our wedding pictures and our marriage certificate, explaining the mistake that they had made. A few days later, we received a letter of apology from the Liverpool old case unit, and a new form for further submissions. We arranged an appointment to hand in the new submissions ourselves at the Liverpool office. Everything was calm and peaceful. Our families wrote their letters of support, confirming that I had family ties in the UK. We got all the required information, and on the appointed day in September 2013 we travelled and delivered our further submissions in Liverpool. What a palaver! We did not stop praying about it. We asked the Lord to give me my stay as our first wedding anniversary gift. That would also enable me to travel, and to see Ghana again after so many years.

Chapter 32

The Lord Told Us To Move On

After our wedding, we asked the Lord what He wanted us to do. We sought the Lord for His direction and became convinced He wanted us to move on. The Lord said He had other places for us to go and share our testimony. It was not an easy decision to share with our church, Elim Camberwell, after a successful wedding and the help from everybody. We prayed about it for a month, but events proved to us that the Lord had spoken. We then wrote a letter to the church. It was hard for the church to lose us. We also felt heavy in our hearts. The senior pastor did not want us to leave but said that he did not want to stand in the way of the Lord, if He was leading. At the end of October 2013, my husband and I were called to the front of the church to be prayed for before we moved on. We had prayed to God for that to happen. We will always cherish the memory of the fellowship and love we shared with everyone at Elim Camberwell. It is our prayer the Lord will continue to bless the church.

At that time, the Elim Church was preparing to move to Rushey Green, near Catford. We went to help Jubilee International Church at Grove Park, where I had attended Bible College. By the time we got there, Sureway International Christian Ministries, a larger Assemblies of God church, had been invited in to mother the Jubilee church. In January 2014, Sureway Jubilee Church started, and we were a part of it. We got to know Pastor Eric Ekuban and his wife Sister Louise, who had been asked to lead the church. They have been a great blessing in our lives. In September 2015, the church at Grove Park was closed down. My husband and I then moved to the mother church, where we are now. We believe that the Lord led us there. For us it is home, and the senior pastor and his wife are a gift from God. Pastor Steve Armah and his wife, Sister Wendy, are honourable servants of the living God, and a pleasure to get to know. My husband and I have made ourselves available for God, to send us wherever He wants us to go, to testify of His wonderful works in our lives.

Chapter 33

Our First Anniversary Gift From The Lord

On the 10ᵗʰ March 2014, I was at home cooking my husband's special dish, peanut butter soup with lamb. He had requested it for our first wedding anniversary. I had opened all the kitchen windows, and one could enjoy the aroma of the soup. I was singing and praising the Lord that day, when I heard the doorbell ring. I went and answered the door. It was the postman. He asked if I was Mrs Rita Vincent. I said yes. He then asked me to sign a recorded delivery letter. When I opened it, it was my stay! (I was granted compassionate leave to remain, initially for two and a half years, after which I could apply to have it extended.) WOW! I started shouting for joy. I lay on the carpet in the living room and rolled and rolled in thanks to God. I couldn't believe my eyes. Since we got married, the Lord had done so many things for us. All we had needed to do was to carry it to the Lord in prayer. He said we should cast all our burdens on Him, for He cares for us. What a living God we serve. He alone deserves all our praise. He did it for me, He will do it for you too.

The Lord also fulfilled the prophecy, given by Bishop Frank Ofosu-Appiah that I would be able to go to Ghana and return. I had received a word of knowledge from the bishop, the founder of Living Springs, who had visited the church from Atlanta, USA. It was the Sunday after my birthday, and I had purposed in my heart to bring a thanksgiving offering to the Lord. During the ministration of God's Word, the Holy Spirit said that I should put the seed offering into the hand of the bishop. I pondered over this, and I thought I would give it to him privately after the service. However, when it was time for the general offering, the bishop announced that everyone should come and put their offering in his hands. When I heard him say that, I felt the manifestation of God's presence. Then the Holy Spirit said to me, this is what I told you to do. It is very important to be sensitive to the presence of God. Whenever we are in church, the Holy Spirit is always there to bring answers to our prayers. The "when" and "how" is for God to decide, what we must do is to be obedient. The offering started, and everyone put their money in the bishop's hand, and as he blessed them, he put the offering into the offering bowl. When it got to my turn, I put my offering in his hand, and he told me to stand aside and wait.

After he had finished with the offering, he came to me and said, "God says your daddy died and left an inheritance for you in Ghana." I replied "Yes." He continued, "And you want to go to Ghana." I replied "Yes." (Though in my mind, I was wondering how I could go to Ghana without my leave to remain.) Then he said, "The Lord says, He will get you your papers, and He will take you to Ghana and bring you back to the UK." I fell on the floor, under the power of the Holy Spirit, in front of the congregation of about four hundred people. Who says God is not in the midst of His people? I was overwhelmed by the experience, and I shouted thank you God, thank you, Lord Jesus, thank you, Holy Spirit. That was the beginning of my deliverance and my immigration breakthrough. I wrote down the word of promise from the Lord which I had received. I believed it, and I started running with it through prayer, confession and trusting God to bring it to pass. I did not remain the same from that day.

"And we know that all things work together for good to them that love God, to them who are called according to His purpose." (Romans 8:28). By the grace of God, my husband and I are a living testimony to the truth of that verse from the Bible. The Lord moved every mountain to bring the prophecy to pass, concerning my marriage, which I had waited 28 years to see fulfilled. It is amazing how God brought me all the way from Nigeria, where I received the prophecy, to Ghana, and then to the UK, to bring us together. "God is not man that He should lie, neither the son of man that he should repent: hath he said, and shall He not do it? Or hath He spoken, and shall He not make it good?" (Numbers 23:19.)

Chapter 34

A Trip To Ghana

A year after I got my stay, we decided to visit Ghana, in fulfilment of the word of the Lord. We started praying about it. We asked the Lord to help us with our plans. I had not been able to travel for eleven years, and we were both excited about everything. Two months before we travelled, I sent a barrel and a box of shopping and gifts to my family and friends, through a shipping agent. All my family back home were glad to hear I was returning, for a holiday with my husband. My elder brother and his family were prepared to host us and sent us an invitation to be submitted in support of my husband's visa application. We chose to fly KLM. We were glad when the barrel and box arrived in Ghana, a week before we travelled on Tuesday 3rd November 2015.

On the evening of the 1st November, we heard the news that Heathrow airport was in chaos because of foggy weather. Most flights were cancelled, and many people were sleeping at the airport. I told my husband that God would make a way for everything to settle down by Tuesday morning, for us to travel. We prayed and trusted the Lord as we sang this song: "The Lord who began it, He will accomplish it. He is the Alpha and Omega, the beginning and the end, He will accomplish it, He will accomplish it." By Tuesday morning, the fog had cleared and our flight departed on time. We had a very good journey and enjoyed our holiday in Ghana. The Lord gave us favour everywhere we visited. Everyone was so pleased to see me, and my husband who had been able to learn some basic words in Akan, the most popular language spoken everywhere. My elder brother made arrangements for us to visit Cape Coast, Elmina and Takoradi. My husband saw, for the first time, the castles on the coast that were used in the slave trade, a harrowing and memorable experience. These towns are in the area that I come from which I had not been to for the past three decades.

We spent a most beautiful night, on our way back to Accra, at Anomabo Beach Resort, where we slept in a mud cabin near the beach. It was my husband's birthday, and it was a joy for him to spend it in Africa, on his first visit there, eating fish and chips with me, looking at the ocean. The fish was tilapia, rather than cod, but he said he enjoyed it just as much! We wished we could stay longer in that beautiful place.

The day after we left the beach resort, we went to see Uncle Tagoe in Winneba. He was the only surviving older relative of my mum. I had not seen him for at least twenty years. Brother Brian, our brother's driver, drove us on our trip along the coast. He took us to Uncle Tagoe's house, but he was not there. My uncle lived down the end of a long dirt road, very rough and steep. We were concerned that the car would not be able to get back up again. While the main roads in Ghana can be good, cars can take a heavy pounding on many of the local roads. When we phoned Uncle Tagoe, we learnt that he was at Peace Radio, a community radio station that he helped to run. Uncle Tagoe had been a newsreader on the television in Ghana for many years and was a well-known figure. I was pleased that the gift I bought for him, a flask, was just what he needed. He showed us around the radio station, and we spent time with him and his family. His grown-up children were also there, as they were visiting him from abroad. He was the last person that we spoke to on our trip to Ghana, calling him shortly before we boarded the plane. My husband was so touched by how charming he was, as my uncle told him how glad he was to see me again and to know that I had found a good husband. Shortly after we returned to the UK, we learnt that Uncle Tagoe had died, following a short illness. It meant so much to me, to have seen him again before he went to be with the Lord.

I was also a great joy to meet old friends, who I hadn't seen for so many years. We visited Sister Doreen and her husband, Brother Victor, one evening. We sat outside, with little light, due to the "Dumsor". (There were regular power cuts at that time in Ghana.) We joked and laughed, and Brother Victor showed us around the Christian school that they owned and taught in. It was open, and doing well, but the building was still being extended. We had to be careful, as we were walking around in the dark.

Sister Doreen told me about another old friend, Deborah, a young woman who I had taken under my wings, when I was living in Ghana. She was going through a difficult time, and I had wanted to help her. I arranged for her to come and work as a cleaner in a salon that Sister Doreen then owned. After I left, Sister Doreen trained her to be a hairdresser. She later got a job in a top salon, in Accra Mall. I went to the Mall with my husband to try to track her down, but we learnt that she was on maternity leave. They kindly gave us her mobile number, and I was able to speak to her and arrange for us to meet. I saw her again, for the first time in twelve years. She told me that she was now married, with children. We also visited Sister Victoria, one of my dearest friends. She danced for joy with us, when we greeted each other on the roof terrace of the hotel where she lived. Our visit gave me the opportunity to return 500 cedis, which she had given me so that I could pay my visa fee all those years before. I knew that she had borrowed the money to be able to give it to me. And I knew she had never expected it to be returned. She hadn't even known if she would see my face again. Truly this lady cast her bread upon the waters and found it again after many days.

We had wonderful opportunities to share our testimony in Ghana, to the glory of God. I shared my testimony in large churches, and people were so excited to hear all that the Lord had done. It was a great joy to go back to Maranatha and speak in both morning services, before hundreds of people. As we entered the church and listened to the preaching which had already started, we were shocked to realise that the pastor was talking about me. He told the story of how I had emptied my bank account and used the money to buy 21 bags of cement. He invited us to come to the front, in the middle of his sermon, and share what had happened in my life since then. The congregation were thrilled to hear my story and rejoiced loudly.

It was a joy to return home to Ghana, after a decade, with my husband, and a new name, Joy. We returned safely to the UK, rejoicing and praising the Lord for His promise, and the fulfilment of it.

Chapter 35

Major Works

Trusting God never comes to an end. The fact that something has been given by God does not mean that there will not be challenges. Indeed, Christ told us that in this life we will have troubles, but to take heart for He had overcome the world. Our faith is expressed in believing that the God who has delivered us before, will surely deliver us again.

One of the new problems that my husband and I had to deal with, after our marriage, came in a letter we opened one morning. We received an estimate, from our freeholder, for forthcoming major works. Our share of the proposed cost was over £15,000. We were aware of our responsibility as leaseholders to pay our share of the cost of major works. But our solicitor did not inform us of impending major works when we purchased. In fact, we knew that the leaseholders on our estate had already faced a large major works bill, not many years before. The person that we bought from had paid £22,000. So we thought that we were safe, and any new works would be much further down the line.

My husband opened the letter, and after a moment of shocked silence read it out to me. We were concerned but did make the decision to trust God and expressed our faith, as we have often done, in song. We put the bill on the kitchen floor and danced around it, singing a favourite song, the one I mentioned when I wrote of my wedding: "Who has the final say? Jehovah has the final say." On many evenings after that we did the same, laying the estimate on the floor of our living room and dancing round it.

That was the start of much frantic activity, working with other leaseholders on the estate. We worked together to challenge the scope of the work and to try to ensure that only necessary work was done. We formed a group, chaired by the leaseholder who lived above us, that met about once a month in our flat. We even paid for a surveyor to look at the work on our behalf, and that was helpful in challenging the work.

Our efforts did bring some success over time: the work went ahead but the scope of the work was reduced, and it was delayed while the reports from the two surveyors were looked at and some compromises were made. The freeholder suggested a working party be established, with several leaseholders on it, as well as tenants, and that group has done a good job. As I write, the work is now done, and we await the final bill.

The estimate was a challenge to our faith, and we debated long and hard about how best to pay the bill. In our own wisdom, we felt the only way forward was to get a lodger. At the very time that we were considering this, an old acquaintance of mine called me, and asked me if I knew anyone who had a room to rent. She needed to move and come to London. As you can imagine, we thought this could only be the hand of God! She came and met with us, and we agreed to rent the room to her. Within a week she made arrangements to move in. She told me that she didn't have many things, as I had told her there wasn't much storage space in our flat. But when she arrived, we were shocked by how many things she brought into the flat. She came with her own car and a van loaded with possessions. As soon as she arrived, we wondered if this arrangement would ever work. That evening, we explained to her that we had put a chair by the side of her bed, and we asked her to sit on that, rather than on the edge of the bed. We realised that she wasn't happy, but we had just bought our beds and the instructions given were not to sit on the edge, as that would damage them.

The next morning, I spoke to her and asked her what her plans were for the day. We asked if she was going out, but she said that she was just resting. We then went to church, as it was Sunday morning. When we returned home, the first thing I noticed was that her car was not there. As we went in, the keys we had given her were on the floor. I picked up the keys and ran into her room, only to find it empty. While we had been out, she had packed up all her possessions and left. She left us a note, with fifteen pounds, saying that she couldn't cope with our harsh rules!

We felt immensely relieved, as if a heavy burden had been lifted. We praised God for our deliverance and went to church the following week and shared the testimony of our one-night lodger. We agreed that we did not want a lodger to share our home. We had recently married and needed to get to know each other better. In the end, we were able to borrow the money. No harm was done, we hope our lodger was happier elsewhere, and we did make fifteen pounds on the deal!

Chapter 36
First Fruits Offering

After my marriage, I tried applying for different jobs, and I took my CV to various places, but did not have any success. Because of that, I decided to register as self-employed, and provide a cleaning and care service. I only had a few customers, and helped them with ironing, cleaning, and sometimes shopping. After a year of self-employment, the problems with my work became ever more apparent to me: I had no paid leave, and my clients often cancelled, as sometimes they were away. In the end, I only had two clients, and had a long journey to one of them. My travel costs were high and so my income was uncertain and limited.

One day, I came home from work and cried out to God. I confessed I was tired of cleaning people's toilets, even my own! I asked God to turn my situation around. I requested better employment: a job with paid leave, and a pension. I believed in my heart that God would deliver me again.

When I told my husband that I did not want to do self-employed work anymore, he took it seriously. He started looking on the internet again for job opportunities. For some time, he had mentioned Waitrose would be a good employer, as they were employee owned, had a good reputation, and paid an annual bonus. So my husband kept an eye on their website, and soon enough we saw a vacancy for a night shift worker, at our local branch. The Beckenham store is only a few minutes, by bus, from our home.

I wanted to apply, but at that time my papers and passport had gone to the Home Office, as I needed an extension to my Discretionary Leave to Remain. I had the right to work but couldn't bring the documents to prove that. It was also difficult for me to provide references. I decided to apply anyway, and trust that God would make a way. The deadline for applications was very close, and as we had a busy weekend we had to apply late on Sunday night. It was a relief to find out the following day that I had been shortlisted. I was offered an interview, in two weeks' time. I went to my interview without my passport, or residence permit, and was relieved to find that they were not asked for. Later, the Home Office confirmed my entitlement to work, with Waitrose.

I was given the job, but only on a short-term contract. I had already ended my self-employment and was concerned about what I would do when my contract at Waitrose ended. But I remembered that it was God who had given me my job. I remembered the word of the Lord in Proverbs chapter 3:9-10: "Honour the Lord with thy substance, and with the first-fruits of all thine increase: So shall thy barns be filled with plenty, and thy presses shall burst out with new wine." I pondered that scripture in my heart and felt that I should honour the Lord with the whole of my first month's salary and trust Him to make a way for me to have permanent work at Waitrose.

One evening, my husband said that he had something he wanted to talk about. He said he believed we should give a first-fruits offering and give my first month's pay to the Lord. As we were agreed, I gave my first-fruits offering as soon as my first month's salary arrived. Whenever my contract was mentioned at Waitrose, I confessed that it would not end, and that my employment was permanent. In the end, instead of my contract ending, I was given the opportunity to work during the day, instead of working nights. That presented a new challenge, as I found myself working in the cold part of the store. This caused problems with my injured little toe which became swollen and painful. I was referred to Occupational Therapy and safeguards were put in place to help. I am now back in the warmer parts of the store, putting out the bread on the shelves.

All the time that I have worked at Waitrose, I have lived up to my new name, Joy! I am known for my singing. When I worked nights, I used to praise the Lord loudly throughout my shift. Nobody seemed to mind. Now I am on days, I sing quietly when customers enter the store. They like to hear me singing and encourage me. I greet people with a smile and enjoy my job. It has been a great blessing, and has helped our finances, and made it easier for us to travel.

My husband has also had to trust God over his employment. The charity he works for has faced severe cuts, and there have been constant changes and often the threat of redundancy. Several times, he has had to re-apply to keep his job. At one point, he had to attend an interview, as part of a re-structure. There was only one post available which would enable him to keep his full-time hours, and six support workers having to re-apply for work. To add to the pressure, he was unwell, off sick with severe headaches due to a blockage in his ear. He couldn't sleep on the night before the interview. He was given the opportunity to postpone the interview but didn't want his colleagues to have to keep waiting.

At that time, he was reading through the whole Bible, using a Bible plan. On the day after the interview, he reached the final Bible reading, including Malachi chapter 3:10-11: "Bring ye all the tithes into the storehouse, that there may be meat in mine house, and prove me herewith, saith the LORD of hosts, if I will not open the windows of heaven, and pour you out a blessing, that there shall not be room enough to receive it. And I will rebuke the devourer for your sakes, and he shall not destroy the fruit of your ground; neither shall your vine cast her fruit before the time in the field, saith the LORD of hosts." A few hours after he had read those verses, he had a call from the Director who conducted the interview. He was told he had scored highest, and so had his first preference: he could keep his full-time hours.

Chapter 37

Israel

It was always the desire of my heart to travel to Israel. But I had never been able to go. For many years, I was not able to leave the UK because of my immigration status. Sometimes, our desires do not seem to be fulfilled, but I can testify that if we stay in the will of God, the good desires in our heart will be satisfied.

In June 2017, I still hadn't heard from the Home Office, following my application for further leave to remain. Around that time, Prophet Ron Jollif and his wife returned to our church. Prophet Ron called my husband and me to the front of the church, while he was ministering, and gave us a word from the Lord. He said he felt that we would go to Israel, and that God would speak to us there. I was so excited, and I knew in my spirit that God had opened the door for us. Within a few days, we heard from the Home Office who granted me further Discretionary Leave. I was free to travel again!

As we both believed the prophecy was from God, we made arrangements to go. We decided to travel independently, rather than join an organised tour. We wanted to experience the Holy Land at our own pace. We found that flying from Luton was a good option for us. Having checked out hotels on the internet, we took the plunge, and booked a hotel in East Jerusalem, the National Hotel. We weren't aware, initially, that the hotel was in the Arab part of the city. We chose the National because it was close to the places we wanted to see. Yet it turned out to be an excellent choice. The area felt friendly and safe, with lots of interesting shops and market stalls. We had a spacious room, with a large bed, leading on to a roof terrace overlooking the area, shared with just a few other rooms. The staff were friendly and helpful.

We felt the presence of the Lord in Israel, and it was a great joy to see the land of the Bible as we visited all the usual attractions: Yad Vashem, Israel's memorial to the victims of the holocaust, the Western Wall, Bethlehem, the Garden Tomb and the Mount of Olives. To stand on the Mount of Olives and look down on the Old City, then go to the Garden of Gethsemane, touched me deeply. I sang, and prayed to God, while I was there. We were also able to visit the south, Masada and the Dead Sea.

When we took our day trip to Masada, we were short of time. My husband had been to Israel more than thirty years before but had never been back. He had volunteered on a Kibbutz, near Tel Aviv. At that time, he did go to the Dead Sea, but forgot to bring his trunks. So he was pleased that this time he would be able to swim. But on the way to the bus station in Jerusalem, he lost a bag containing his trunks and we were delayed. I was determined to get to the Dead Sea before we had to return on the bus. The buses were not frequent. We had a memorable but hurried visit to Masada, travelling up to the famous ruins, dating from the days of Herod the Great, in the cable car.

After we left, having come down again, we walked down the steep slope to the entrance. We could see that a man was waiting for us. We had just asked a lady in the shop, selling beauty products, if we could still get to the Dead Sea in time to swim. I still wanted my Dead Sea mud! She mentioned that the nearest place was Ein Bokek, although it was too far to walk. So it seemed helpful, initially, that the man waiting for us turned out to be a taxi driver, and immediately offered to take us there.

We were unhappy, though, with the way that he went about it, hassling us into his cab, before we had time to think. He insisted that we must go immediately. We asked for the price, and he told us thirty-five shekels. He then drove us from Masada, into more of the barren desert that we had travelled through, on our way down from Jerusalem. We only saw the occasional car and had no idea how far it was to Ein Bokek. The taxi driver then asked us to pay the fare, although the journey had just started. He said we must pay seventy shekels, as that was the price for two people. We argued with him and declined to pay. He became belligerent, threatening to stop the cab, and leave us to walk through the desert. As we gave him our thirty-five shekels, he pretended he would throw the money out of the window. I prayed in tongues, loudly, to my husband's embarrassment. I told the driver that God was watching him. He suddenly went quiet, and agreed to take us to Ein Bokek, for the original price. (The incident reminded me that the devil came to the Lord when he was in the desert.) I did get to float in the Dead Sea, and I got my mud, though I bought it in the end.

It was a great joy to spend a day with my daddy-in-law, during our stay. He travels to Israel often, as he is the UK representative of a ministry based in the north of the country. This ministry, Sabra, helps to care for the poor and needy, including some holocaust survivors. It also helps people to make Aliyah and return to the land of their fathers: (Aliyah is a term used to describe the return of Jewish people to Israel, from wherever they live in the world). Sabra is a bridge between Christians and Jews, and a blessing to many. My mother-in-law, who died before I met my husband, was also involved with Sabra for many years. We had the privilege of visiting a synagogue and meeting an Orthodox rabbi who had known her well. He showed us the memorial for her on the synagogue wall. The rabbi also showed us the Torah scrolls and encouraged my husband to hold one.

I finally met Brother Moti Klimer, a man of God with a tremendous testimony, who founded Sabra and leads the ministry. We met him, with my daddy-in-law, in Afula, where Sabra is based. I had heard a great deal about him. He greeted me and asked if it was my first visit to Israel. When I said that it was, he remarked that I had been given a privilege that even Moses had been denied! Brother Moti showed me around Sabra house. I also saw the view from the back garden: the valley of Megiddo, where the battle of Armageddon will take place one day. We saw the word of the Lord, given by Prophet Ron, being fulfilled, as Brother

Moti talked to us about Sabra, and asked us to become more involved. He said he hoped we would come back one day. We would love to do that and to help in any way we can.

Chapter 38

Dad's Tenth Anniversary Celebration

Having missed my father's funeral, it was a blessing to travel, with my husband, back to Ghana, to attend the ten-year commemoration of his death. This event took place in January 2018. We stayed in Lashibi, with my brother Gilbert and my sister-in-law Ellen. They have a beautiful home and are so welcoming.

Very early one morning, we drove to the cemetery and met our relatives and friends at the entrance. We all dressed in white. We were able to walk to the grave before the heat of the day was too strong. On my last trip back to Ghana, we had tried to find my father's grave, with Brother Gilbert, but couldn't do so. There is little order in the Accra cemetery, and a vast number of graves. It is precarious walking there. You have step from grave to grave, and in the narrow spaces between them, being careful not to miss your footing. But since our visit, the grave had been found, and beautifully prepared for the celebration, by my brother Atta. After some hymns and prayers, led by a Methodist minister, we all sprayed perfume on the grave, as is the custom in Ghana.

We had a wonderful stay, and I had the opportunity to see Deborah again. This time, we came to her home, and met her husband and children. I was so excited to meet her new baby, Rita Joy, who she had named after me. It is a big honour in Ghana, to have a child named after you. I had my hair done at her house, which took the best part of the day. My husband sat outside, at the front of the house, watching people, chickens, hens, cars, cats and dogs go by. We brought a Beginner's Bible, for Rita Joy, and pray that she will grow up to love the word of God. We also had the honour of giving one to my great niece, baby Samantha, who we met for the first time. She is the daughter of my dear nephew Fifi and his beautiful wife Irene.

We went to Cape Coast again, to visit my friend Sister Esther. You may remember that I lived with her for six months, many years ago. I hadn't seen her for twenty-seven years. The baby I had helped to care for was now a young lady, a seamstress, who mended some clothes for me. We had the pleasure of going to the beach and walking beside the ocean with Sister Esther's son. It was a pleasure to see the fishermen, helped by the women, pulling in the catch together. The baited nets are left to lie in the water, far out from the beach. It takes a long time, and much effort, to pull them in again. The beach was lined by coconut and palm trees.

I was able to see Sister Doreen and her husband. We went to their Christian school and met the children and teachers. My husband is amazed how smart and well-behaved school children are in Ghana. I saw two schools on the trip, as we went with my brother Gilbert to Lake Volta, where we saw the famous dam, and visited a private school, Legacy Girl's College in Akuse. My sister-in-law and brother have been instrumental in founding that school. It was a joy to see so many monkeys, by the side of the road, as we drove to the lake Volta region.

Only three weeks after we returned from Ghana, we flew back again. We had received an invitation to a wedding a few months before. I had so much wanted to go, but I didn't think it would be possible for us to return so quickly. Yet God made a way. Not only financially, but he enabled us to travel despite appalling weather in London. We had to go to an internet café to check in for our flight, and there was thick snow on the ground. The day before we flew, Matthew was still working, travelling around London as the snow came down. It was an act of faith to go to the airport, as many flights were cancelled. We stayed the night at the Premier Inn, Heathrow, and got up early to check in. As we were getting ready, in our hotel room, my husband received a text from KLM: to our relief, our flight was not cancelled. We had been re-booked, onto a direct flight with British Airways. We had been due to change in Amsterdam. Our plane was de-iced before take-off, but we stepped into the intense heat of Ghana, only a few hours behind schedule.

The wedding invitation was from Rita Akumiah, the daughter of Sister Victoria, to whom I had returned the 500 cedis. Like Rita Joy, she was named after me. We stayed one night back in Lashibi and then flew to Kumasi, the garden city, the next day. We spent the next five nights staying with Sister Victoria, her other children, and her sisters. We also had the chance to see something of the Ashanti region: Lake Bosomtwe, just an hour's drive from Kumasi, the museum at the Palace of the Ashanti king, the Cultural Centre and the Central Market. Even I, a Ghanaian, was amazed by how vast and crowded the market was. We bought kente cloths there. You could barely squeeze by all the people, in the narrow lanes of the market, to get to all the different stalls.

I gave the Lord a good dance at Rita's wedding. Having read my book this far, you should know me by now! Matthew joined me to dance as we rejoiced, in the service at the large Pentecostal church, and at the reception at the Golden Bean Hotel. Let me tell you the story of why Rita was named after me. I hadn't seen her for over twenty years, before we met again for her wedding. She lives in the US. We had always kept in contact, speaking on the phone, but never been able to meet. When I was young, her father had loved me, and wanted to marry me, but my dad would not give his permission. Later, he married Sister Victoria and had children, including Rita. He decided that she would be named after me. I love Sister Victoria, and my husband also admires her deeply. You see, she could have hated me, resented my presence in her life, and the life of her daughter. Instead, she became a great friend, and did so much to help me while I still lived in Ghana. Her husband died some time ago, and things have not been easy for her. I know in my heart, that just as she has always been there for me, I will be there for her, as long as we both live on this earth.

Chapter 39

God Makes All Things Beautiful In His Time

I did not have a purpose in life, until the grace of God found me and gave me hope through our Saviour, the Lord Jesus Christ. The Lord watched over me, so that I did not die before I had time to fulfil my destiny. When I was in secondary school, I could have drowned during our school fun day at the seaside. The waves were strong, while I was playing at the edge of the sea, and they carried me away. God sent His angels to deliver me. I did not know how I was brought to safety, but I opened my eyes and found myself in hospital. The nurse who stood by me told me I had been unconscious for two days.

Ten years later, in October 1985, came the beginning of my deliverance and calling to become a child of God. I have learnt through the years it is not about me. I have learnt that if I focus on my calling, and fulfil my destiny, that will also benefit others. For example, in coming to the UK to help care for my two nieces, and to get married to my darling husband, I helped to fulfil God's plan for their lives. God in His infinite wisdom had linked our destinies together.

Suffering in Christ is part of our discipleship. There is nothing strange about it. But faithful is He that calls us. It is acceptable to cry out to God during the trials that we go through, as He prepares us to receive a greater testimony. "No test, no testimony!" I cried alone to the Father, Son and Holy Spirit. I sought the wisdom and understanding of God, as I waited patiently for an answer. He was working behind the scenes on my behalf, when I thought that He was silent. In the end, my cry was heard and answered. When the Lord turned my mourning into dancing, my husband and everybody danced with me. As the saying goes, "When you cry, you cry alone, but when you laugh, the world laughs with you." In His time, God makes all things beautiful, against all the odds. For with God all things are possible.

The Lord Jehovah is His Name. In the words of the song, "What He said He would do, that is what He has done." Amen.

Chapter 40

I Must Preach The Gospel

My story started with how I was born a smiling baby. It is only in Christ that I have lived to see myself smiling daily, with the joy of the Lord which is my strength. Giving my life to God, through the knowledge of the Gospel of Christ, made all the difference. I am not ashamed to preach the same Gospel to you, "For it is the power of God unto salvation to everyone that believeth." (Romans 1:16) The experience of being born again is open to all. (John 3:3) If you have not yet accepted the Lord Jesus as your personal Saviour, this is your time and the day of your salvation. Please pray this prayer aloud wherever you are: "Father in Heaven, thank you for sending your Son to suffer for my sake. I believe He died, and rose again on the third day. I am a sinner and I have sinned against you. I surrender my life to you, and I ask you to forgive me for all my sins. I accept the gift of your Son, as my Lord and Saviour. Lord Jesus, come and dwell in me by your Holy Spirit, and help me to live a life pleasing in your sight. Thank you, Father, in the name of the Lord Jesus I pray. Amen." If you have prayed sincerely, trust that God has heard you. The good news is that you are born again. As a new-born child of God, your daily milk is reading the Holy Bible. Start reading the Gospel of John and the book of Romans, which will explain more about your new birth. Ask God to lead you to a Spirit filled, Bible believing church, and He will. Thank you.

About the Author

Rita C. Joy and Matthew Vincent live in London. With the blessing of their former church, Rita and Matthew have recently joined Catford AOG, which is in their local area. This church is led by Pastor Lunga and his wife Sister Thanda from South Africa. Rita is passionate about evangelism, prayer, bible study, preaching and dancing.

She was born in Ghana and spent her early years in Ghana and Nigeria. She attended a bible school in Lagos, at Winners' chapel, and later an AOG bible school, South London Christian College. She is an excellent speaker, and has shared her testimony at large churches, in the UK and Ghana. She has had opportunities to preach, and minister to women. Rita is known, amongst both Christians and non-Christians, as a woman of faith and joy. She currently works at Waitrose, Beckenham, where she enjoys singing praises to the Lord as she works.

Rita and Matthew married in 2013, in Elim Camberwell: their wedding was attended by over four hundred people, forcing many to stand outside. Rita has faced tremendous challenges in her life, and has seen the faithfulness of God.

BV - #0051 - 300523 - C0 - 216/138/9 - PB - 9781913181864 - Gloss Lamination